Tracking Training for All Dogs

From the First Track to a
Successful Trial Experience

Ute Fallscheer

Dogwise Publishing

Wenatchee, Washington U.S.A.

Tracking Training for All Dogs
From the First Track to a Successful Trial Experience
Ute Fallscheer

Dogwise Publishing
A Division of Direct Book Service, Inc.
403 South Mission Street, Wenatchee, Washington 98801
1-509-663-9115, 1-800-776-2665
www.dogwisepublishing.com / info@dogwisepublishing.com
© 2024 Franckh-Kosmos-Verlags-GmbH & Co.

Interior and cover design: Lindsay Davisson

Limits of Liability and Disclaimer of Warranty
The author and publisher shall not be liable in the event of incidental or consequential damages in connection with, or arising out of, the furnishing, performance, or use of the instructions and suggestions contained in this book.

Library of Congress Cataloging-in-Publication Data

Names: Fallscheer, Ute, author.
Title: Tracking training for all dogs : from the first track to a
    successful trial experience / Ute Fallscheer.
Description: Wenatchee, Washington U.S.A. : Dogwise Publishing, [2024] |
    Includes index. | Summary: "This is a reference book for professionals
    and people experienced with tracking as well as a structured guide for
    beginners. In particular, it includes a list of possible training
    mistakes, their interpretation, and advice on how to correct them to
    ensure success. For readers with no experience, the book is an easy to
    follow introduction"-- Provided by publisher.
Identifiers: LCCN 2024036415 | ISBN 9781617812903 (paperback)
Subjects: LCSH: Tracking dogs. | Dogs--Training--Handbooks, manuals, etc. |
    Dogs--Obedience trials--Tracking.
Classification: LCC SF428.75 .F35 2024 | DDC 636.7/0886--dc23/eng/20241029
LC record available at https://lccn.loc.gov/2024036415

ISBN: 9781617812903   Printed in the U.S.A.

Table of Contents

Foreword by Michael Tomczak

For at least 15,000 years, the dog has had a special place as a companion. Due to his extraordinary abilities and loyalty, the *Canis lupus familiaris* was the first animal to be domesticated by humans and developed into an indispensable helper and friend.

The promotion and development of working dogs and especially tracking dogs is a cultural asset that is preserved and promoted by many dog sports enthusiasts.

When Ute asked me to write this foreword, I immediately agreed. After reviewing the manuscript, I was thrilled. At last, a contemporary and competent handbook for training in the field of tracking with dogs and for training tracking dogs.

This is a reference book for professionals and people experienced with tracking as well as a structured guide for beginners. In particular, it includes a list of possible training mistakes, their interpretation, and advice on how to correct them to insure success. For readers with no experience, the book is an easy to follow introduction.

Ute and I both hope that the community of dog lovers will make this work their own for the training of tracking dogs and that the user will be successful in training tracking dogs.

Michael Tomczak, Sprockhövel, 28.08.2019

- Multiple World Champion FCI IPO FH (Single, Team)
- Runner-up World Champion FCI IPO FH
- Multiple German Champion VDH IPO FH
- Frequent participant in World Championships (FCI) and German Championships (VHD and dhv)

Michael Tomczak with Aik vom Rio Negro at the World Chamionpships.

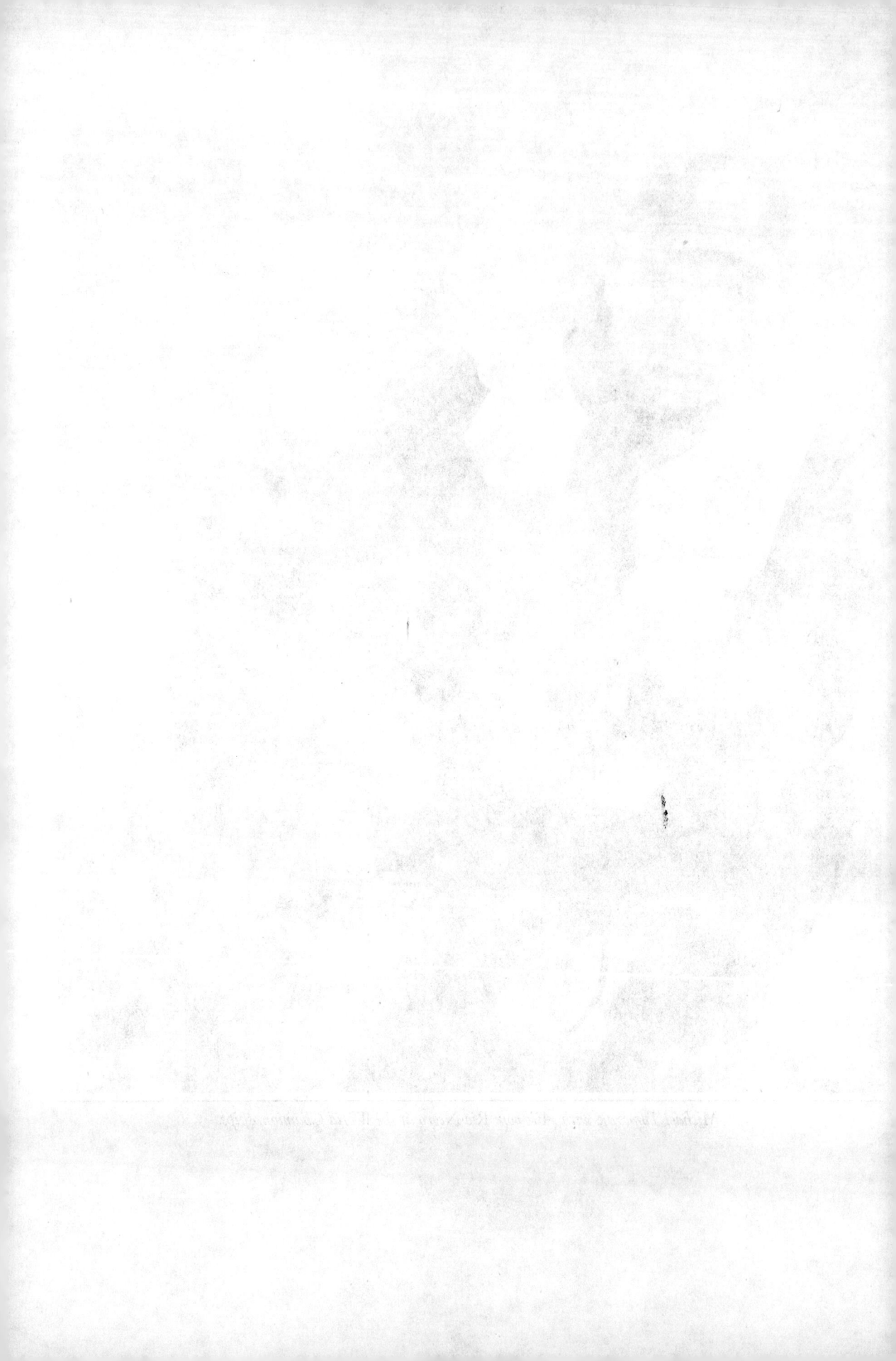

Introduction

It's bitterly cold. A hard-frozen brown field. The biting cold and the wind bring tears to my eyes. I can hardly see my dog in front of me. She walks with her nose deep on the ground following a track, which I do not see and which, from my perspective, she actually can no longer track in these weather conditions. However, suddenly my dog walks toward me. We failed, I think to myself, because we are in the middle of a tracking trial, but then I realize that she has her nose down, sniffing intensively and continuing consistently just past me. She is still on the track! I can hardly believe how she tracks and finds the track; I am fascinated and thrilled to see her skills. Finally, I stand in front of the spectators in tears and hear the evaluation: 98 of 100 possible points,

Beginner training on a track laid out on flat terrain.

the qualification as a substitute starter for the World Championship. All achieved by a small Border Terrier. An unforgettable moment!

Such moments are unique, but repeat themselves again and again on a smaller scale during tracking training. It is fascinating what a dog can perceive and accomplish with his nose. Anyone who sees a tracking dog at work is impressed by how focused he follows the track, despite several hours having passed between the laying of the track and the actual tracking. No wonder the sport of tracking has more and more followers. Whether you do this sport alone or as part of a training group, the relationship with your dog becomes more intense through training. Furthermore, training is a chance to concentrate on track work with the dog and to forget, for a while, the stressful daily life many of us have.

What Happens During Tracking Work?

Let's briefly look at what a dog does when tracking. It all starts with a track layer who walks across a field or meadow. Using technical jargon, this means: He lays a track. First, he marks the beginning of the track with a rod. Then he walks across the terrain.

In the process, he crushes the vegetation of the terrain or soil crumbs. This creates different smells from

A track is laid on natural terrain.

the parts of the ground that the track layer has not stepped on. However, the tracker does not just walk straight ahead, but changes direction several times and puts several articles on the track. After some time, a handler leads his dog to the beginning of the track. The dog takes up the smell of the stepped on soil at the starting point of the track and can therefore follow the route of the track. He always has his nose close to the ground.

A well-trained tracking dog stays directly on the track despite the changes of direction and does not let himself be diverted from the track even by wind and weather. He finds the articles and indicates them to the handler by lying down, sitting or standing in front of them.

A track can be laid on all natural soils, e.g., a field that has not been sown, sown green field, meadow or forest soil. Depending on the terrain, a track is easier or harder for the dog to track. Those who wish, can compete with other dog handler-dog teams in tracking work and participate in the numerous trials offered.

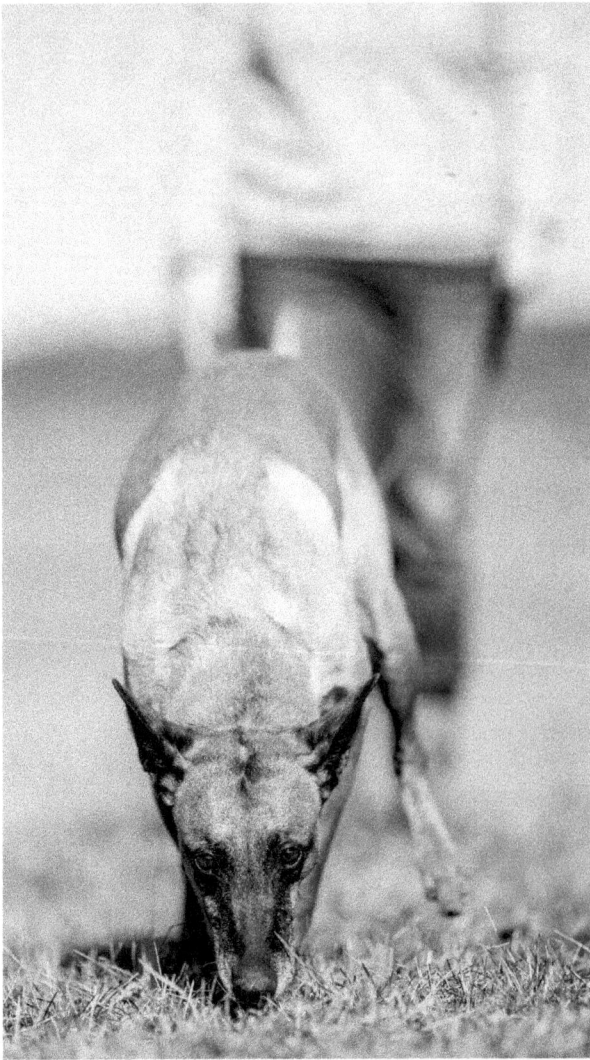

The dog learns to track with a deep nose.

Suitable for All Dogs

Tracking work is exhausting for the dog, even if it doesn't look like it at first. Nose-work challenges the whole dog, both in his physical performance and in his ability to concentrate. Despite all the effort, dogs are extremely motivated to work the track if the training is set up properly. They love doing it.

Tracking work was a part of the former utility dog training for working dogs. For a long time, therefore, only special breeds of dogs, such as German and Belgian shepherds, Hovawarts, Giant Schnauzers, Airedale Terriers, among others, were trained in tracking work. Now, tracking work is not only a part of a utility dog trial but also a dog sport all its own. For some years now, dogs of all breeds, including mixed-breed dogs, have been successfully trained as tracking dogs. Nowadays, successful tracking training always means to adapt the training to the particular dog. Therefore, in this book, you will not only find the description of proven methods for training a tracking dog, but also the theoretical principles behind these methods. This allows you to adapt the training to your dog and independently plan your training.

Dog indicating an article by laying down independently.

The Structure of This Book

This book was written to describe to dog handlers the process of training a tracking dog but also to explain in which cases this process is useful and why. That way the dog handler can react appropriately toward their dogs in different training situations.

When a dog handler knows and applies the basics of dog training and then the specifics of tracking training, they can avoid unnecessary missteps during training sessions.

A central element of this book is to focus on training track. It often determines the quality of the training. How do you sensibly lay a track without over- or under-challenging the dog? What is difficult about a track, and what is easy when the dog is working the track? The younger the dog, the more carefully the handler must consider how to lay the training track. The training track should be laid in such a way that the dog can find it as faultlessly as possible.

The structure of the book follows the logical structure of the training: interesting facts about tracking training in general; the basics of training; the process used during training sessions; laying the training track, corrections during training sessions and, last but not least, trial preparation as well as case studies and many examples. One chapter focuses on trouble-shooting and the use of corrections to avoid behaviors that you don't want. You might notice that some topics are repeated throughout the book. That is because those topics are important fundamentals that show up in different contexts during tracking training.

Last, but not least, the masculine form used in this book always refers to female, male, and diverse persons at the same time. For the sole purpose of better readability, gender-specific spelling and multiple designations are not used. All personal designations are therefore to be understood as gender-neutral.

Have fun reading and then training with your dog.

All the best,

Ute Fallscheer

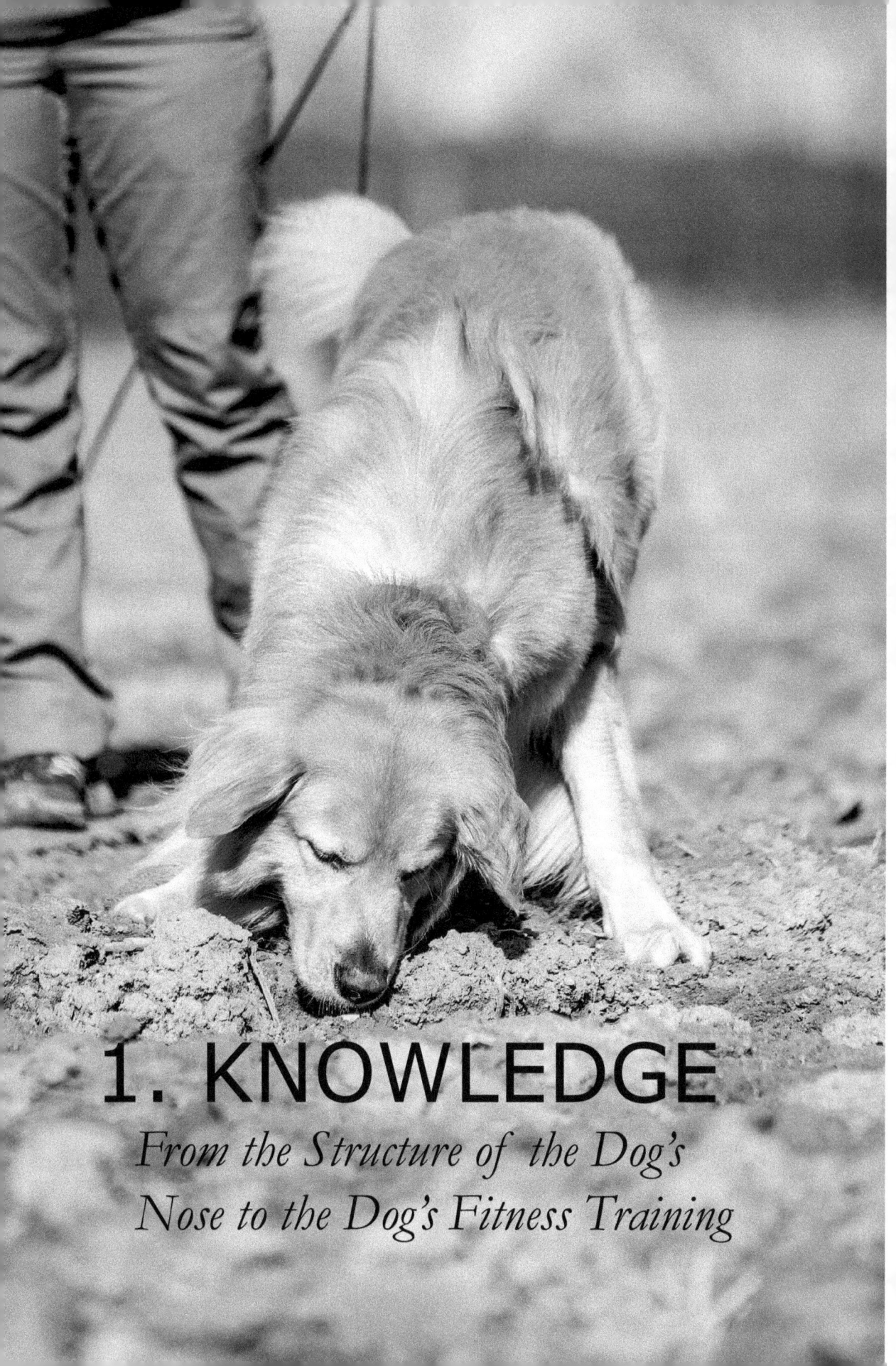

1. KNOWLEDGE

*From the Structure of the Dog's
Nose to the Dog's Fitness Training*

ALL ABOUT TRACKING WORK

When tracking, the dog primarily uses his nose. As humans, it is difficult for us to imagine how sensitive a dog's nose is to smells. It is true that we humans can also smell the difference between a grass field that has not been mowed and a freshly mowed one. However, we cannot smell the difference between a grass field that was walked on and one that has not been walked on.

> *Nothing is more practical than a good theory. - Todor Kaman*

For tracking training, it is important that you have an idea of how and what a dog smells, so you and your dog can become an effective team. Furthermore, since every dog has his own personality, shaped by his breed among other things, this book also dedicates one section to this topic. This chapter is rounded off with important information on health care for a tracking dog and legal aspects of tracking training. After all, most of your training is not on your own property, but on the fields and meadows of private or public land owners. Read this section before you get into trouble with the farmer or hunting leaseholder on whose land you are training with your dog.

The Nose - Breathing, Smelling, Sniffing, Panting

As already mentioned, the most important organ of a dog when searching is his nose. In addition to the vital function of absorbing oxygen through the nose, it warms the inhaled air, humidifies it and filters it. Furthermore, a dog perceives his environment very strongly through the nose. Compared to human olfactory performance, a dog can perceive much finer odors and differences in smells. These smells of the environment have a

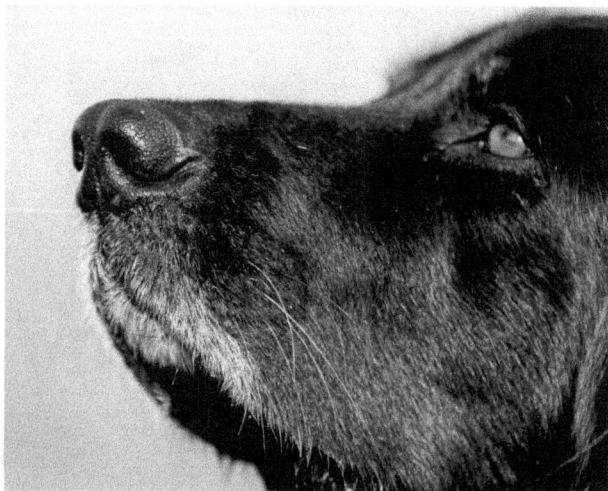

A dog's nose: up to 500 million olfactory cells

very great importance for the dog. They provide it with information about other dogs, food opportunities, and much more.

We humans cannot directly perceive these odor impressions that our dogs perceive. We only see the effects of these olfactory impressions on our dog's behavior. This means for tracking work: A dog handler does not smell what his dog smells. And what the handler sees is not what the dog smells.

This can mean that a track that the handler can see well may be very difficult for the dog to smell and vice versa. Therefore, a handler can only assess what his dog can smell through reflection and professional knowledge. Ultimately, a handler can only see from his dog's reaction whether a place has an odor that the dog can smell. But how does this happen and what is the connection between breathing and smelling?

Breathing

First, the nose serves to inhale and exhale air. The air passes the moist nasal mucus and finally reaches the lungs. This supplies the body with oxygen. Also, exhalation occurs mostly through the nose where the dog exhales used air, thus, CO_2.

Smelling

During the breathing process, odor particles that are in the air are inhaled. Approximately 2% of the normally inhaled air reaches nasal areas in which olfactory cells are located and that can bind the odor particles in the air. The signal triggered in the olfactory cells is transmitted to the brain where it is processed. A dog's ability to smell is greatly reduced when the nasal mucosa dries out. Not only does a dog have a much larger number of olfactory cells than a human, but the evaluation of the information from the olfactory cells in the brain is much more detailed than in humans. Thus, the sensitivity of a dog to smell is much greater than in humans and a dog perceives much finer differences in smell than a human.

But even for the sensitive nose of a dog, the odor molecules in the air must have a certain concentration so the dog can perceive them. This concentration of odor molecules in a track depends, among other things, on the track terrain and the weather. The development of olfactory sensitivity to specific odors can be particularly supported in adolescence. This olfactory sensitivity can be taken advantage of in the dog's tracking training by laying tracks in different terrains early on. For a young inexperienced dog, the track must be very easy to follow if on an unknown novel terrain. He should get to know the new scents and scent differences and not be distracted by additional difficulties.

The dog searches a track that a human often cannot see.

The dog has another olfactory organ in the area of the palate: the vomeronasal organ. This can identify pheromones, intraspecific messengers. The signals of the vomeronasal organ are perceived subconsciously and trigger emotions in the dog. These are, for example, scents of a female dog in heat or signal substances in the urine, which provide information about attraction and aversion as well as social contacts.

If your dog chatters his teeth while sniffing the roadside, he has probably perceived the scent of a female dog in heat through the vomeronasal organ and is therefore aroused. This can strongly distract him from doing his tracking work. He needs to learn to continue tracking despite any possible distractions.

Sniffing

In addition to normal breathing, in which a dog inhales and exhales through both the nose and the mouth, a dog can increase his olfactory perception by sniffing. By sniffing, the odor molecules reach more olfactory cells in the upper areas of the nose. This makes the nose even more sensitive to odors. The dog inhales the air in short puffs through the nose, moves it back and forth in the nose several times, and exhales it in bursts through the nose. Interestingly, the nature of sniffing respiration changes depending on the concentration of odor molecules. At a very low concentration (very fine odor), exhalation occurs through the mouth. This causes the odor molecules to accumulate on the nasal mucosa. An open mouth can therefore be an indication of a particularly intensive search on a challenging track. If, on the other hand, the concentration is high (possibly a strong odor), the dog exhales through the nose in a jerky manner, thereby clearing his nose.

When sniffing, jerky movements of the respiratory muscles are often observed.

Panting

Sniffing is not to be confused with panting. Panting serves to adjust the dog's temperature. When panting, the air flows mostly through the mouth during inhalation and exhalation, and the saliva evaporates. This causes the dog to cool his body temperature. A dog cannot sniff and pant at the same time. During the dog's physical exertion, and the thereby necessarily lowering of the body temperature by panting, the sniffing frequency and thus the olfactory performance of a dog decreases.

Keeping The Nose Healthy

The nose is a very important organ for the health of the dog. It must not be damaged by training. Terrain with toxic or respiratory irritating vapors is unsuitable for training. They accumulate in the dog's nose and may be absorbed by the organism.

The dog's nose should be moist. In very hot weather, after the dog indicates an

The dog can breath, smell, pant, sniff.

article, the nose can be moistened with a cloth. The respiratory muscles especially along the neck should be regularly checked for tension and massaged. The handler should know the breathing sounds that his or her dog makes during intensive tracking. Significant deviations from this can be indications of respiratory diseases. In very hot weather, the dog's ability to smell should be expected to be reduced, as well as if the dog is not in good physical condition.

An open mouth, without the dog slightly raising his nose, is not a sign of superficial tracking. It indicates a particularly intensive track on very difficult tracks or an urgently needed temperature compensation. At mid summertime, the training should be done in the early hours of the day. It is not advised to train in the late evening, especially on terrain without vegetation, as the soil will have gotten very hot throughout the day.

If an unneutered male dog has to track, contact with female dogs in heat is to be avoided or trained. His physical reactions to the scent, including urine, of a female dog in heat cannot be controlled by him. But he can learn to track intensively and concentrate to work despite arousal.

The Scent of the Track

What does the dog smell when it tracks? What distinguishes a ground that has not been trodden on from one that has been trodden on? What happens when a handler lays a track?

The starting point is a terrain with smells of various kinds: the smells of different plants, of different soil organisms, of the droppings of various animals, of rotting plants, of scampering mice, and much more. In addition, the wind carries scents from distant places into the tracking area and vice versa. Then the person laying the track enters the area and lays the track. In doing so, he changes the structure; among other things he compacts the ground, tramples plants and smallest living beings. The result is an injury to the ground under his shoes, sometimes visible and sometimes invisible. These are all processes that set chemical processes in motion, which are associated with an altered odor formation (decomposition processes).

Trodden-on Soil Smells Different Than Non-trodden-on Soil

This applies to all natural soils. In contrast, surfaces made of tar or concrete do not change when walked on. That is why they are unsuitable for tracking work.

In addition to this change of odor due to the change of chemical processes in the trodden ground, the person laying the track releases the smallest particles (skin flakes, sweat particles, etc.) to the environment, some of which sink to the ground. These particles characterize the individual scent of the person. Also, the dog handler's shoes release very small particles through abrasion.

In the midst of this mixture of different odor molecules, the dog is supposed to find the special smell of a trodden track and follow this smell. During this process, the dog can only perceive the odor particles that are in the air, are inhaled and reach the olfactory cells. Since air is usually in motion (e.g., due to wind or thermal processes), the odor molecules also move. This must always be taken into account when interpreting the dog's behavior when tracking.

What the Dog Should Search

A tracking dog should follow the exact route of the track during tracking work. Even if the track can sometimes be seen, he should not track with his eyes, but with his nose. To do this, he must use the developed decomposition odor as an orientation. The individual scent of a human being, which is searched by rescue dogs, is not suitable for exact tracking, since it is usually located away from the tracks due to the influence of the wind.

In tracking dog training, however, we can never rule out the possibility that the dog will also orient himself to the individual scent of the human along the track. Therefore, close observation of the dog's behavior on the track is important. The handler should pay close attention to the dog learning to examine each footfall carefully. This way he will learn not to follow the scent of the person who laid the track, which is often located next to the actual track.

Unfortunately, the odor molecules of the decomposition processes also move away from the track in windy conditions. However, the concentration of these particles is greatest directly above the shoe print in the ground and decreases with distance from the footfall. When training with food on the track, the dog quickly learns that the food is only in the places where the odor concentration is highest. Through this experience, the dog will exactly follow the footsteps during successful training. The closer the odor molecules are together in the air, the easier it is for the dog to smell them.

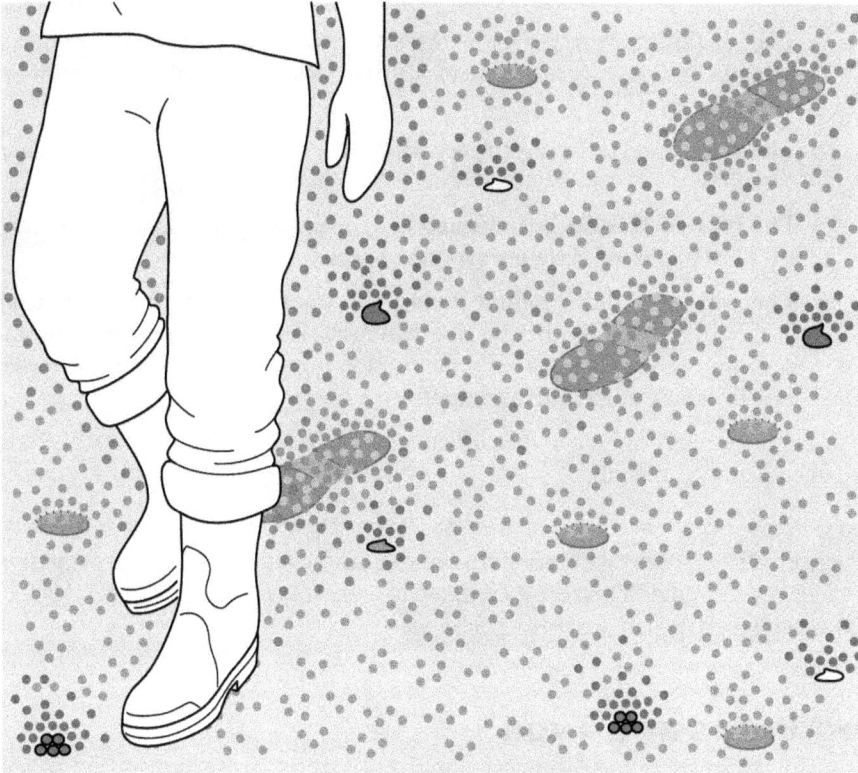

Decomposition odor that the dog should track

Individual odor

Shoe scuff

Mouse holes

Rabbit droppings

Ground odor when there is no wind

The dog should be able to track a variety of odors.

Factors Affecting Scents

There are several factors that contribute to how much odor molecules are released into the air from the terrain and from the decomposition processes, and how they are distributed in the air:

- **The humidity in the air.** Heavy rain captures the odor molecules and transports them back to the ground.

- **The wind direction and strength.** The odor particles are in the air and must be able to be inhaled. Wind causes them to move away from the steps.

- **The air temperature.** A high air temperature as well as a very low air temperature (frost) affect the chemical processes in the soil, fewer odor molecules are released.

- **The time since entering the terrain.** The decomposition processes change over time.

- **The type of terrain.** A cultivated field, meadow, sandy soil, and loamy soil are all examples of different types of terrain.

- **The way of walking when laying the track.** The stronger the changes in the ground caused by the dog handler's treading or shuffling, the more decomposition processes are set in motion that the dog can smell more easily (see air temperature and humidity).

These factors directly influence the difficulty of a track and must always be considered when planning training.

> As humans, we only perceive the visible part of a track. Through knowledge, observation and a lot of experience, a handler can get an idea of what his dog smells when tracking.

Dog Breed and Type

Successful tracking training is always tailored and adapted to the individual dog. Every dog has his own personality and disposition. One is naturally self-confident and curious, the other one cautious and reserved. One approaches life consistently, without caring much about his handler. Another dog cares deeply about his handler and is less interested in tracking. There are breed-typical behaviors, but these can be masked by individual character traits of a dog. A hunting dog that is actually independent by breed can be insecure and dependent by personality. Nevertheless, it is good for the handler to know the breed-typical behavior of a dog, and then to consider the respective dog's individual dispositions. Of course, these considerations also apply to dogs in which several breeds are combined.

Border Terrier and German Shepherd

Let's take a Border Terrier and a German Shepherd as examples. In the case of the Terrier, his breeding emphasizes independent working. He should go independently into a foxhole and drive the fox out. A shepherd dog, on the other hand, should pay attention to the auditory signals of his handler and obey them, and thus, for example, keep a flock of sheep together and lead them. But even within the breeds mentioned, there are great differences in the behavior of individual dogs. Felix, a border terrier, for example, has a strong bond with his handler and orientates himself strongly to her even during a walk. When working, he has a strong will to work and great stamina. When he is tracking, he is not easily distracted. He combines typical breed behavior with a personality that makes working together easier.

Introverted and Extroverted

As you can see, the nature of a dog is shaped by his breed and by his personality. As with humans, there are introverted and extroverted dogs. In training, for example, introverted dogs are usually more sensitive to reprimands than extroverted dogs. Therefore, in training, each dog must be carefully observed to see what effect the individual exercises have on him, and how he can best be trained according to his disposition.

Although only about 21% of dog behavior is determined by genes, knowledge of how breed-specific behavior impacts tracking is very important. Just think of an extroverted hunting dog whose prey-catching behavior when following a game spoor is characterized by a 'high' nose. In tracking work, on the other hand, he should keep his nose close to the ground in every situation. When stressed, i.e., when challenges arise, he is likely to revert to his typical breed behavior. Therefore, one must ensure during training that the dog does not get into stressful situations, especially at the beginning of training, where the handler must constantly deal with the high nose and intervene.

Position of the Tail

The position of the tail during tracking also varies from dog to dog. A raised tail of one dog indicates a strong willingness to work, while of another dog it indicates distraction while tracking. It is worthwhile to closely observe the changes in the tail position during tracking work. For many dogs, the tail lowers as the difficulty of the track increases or as fatigue grows. By closely observing the position of the tail, you will gain valuable information about your dog's physical condition, his motivation, and the difficulty of the track. On the next two pages are a series of photos showing tail position while tracking of a variety of dog breeds.

Do You Know Your Dog?

How do you rate him? Is he rather emotionally stable (influenced by genes, hormones or by special socialization experiences in the first weeks of life), sociable, open to new experiences, extro/introverted, persistent/conscientious, stubborn or similar? What can this mean for training?

Slightly lowered and wagging tail.

Intensive tracking with raised tail.

Health Care for the Tracking Dog

Let us first consider the health effects of tracking. Tracking means fun and effort for the dog at the same time. Through training, the dog's fitness is promoted and increased, especially in the area of concentration. However, dogs are similar to humans. An intensive activity, which requires a lot of concentration and a constant body posture, affects many different parts of the body with increasing duration and intensity of the training.

Impact on Posture

First, let's look at the posture of the dog while tracking. The dog should track continuously with a low nose. Due to the lowered head, the shoulder area of the dog is stressed, both the muscles and tendons as well as the skeletal apparatus. This leads, in some dogs, to a so-called loose shoulder, an instability, which is unfortunately sometimes negatively noted at shows. This possible instability should also be taken into account both in everyday life and in dog sports and treated with physiotherapy if need be so that long-term damage can be avoided. In addition to the shoulder, the elbow joints are also significantly stressed. Furthermore, the musculature around the neck is strongly strained by the bent posture. When tracking, the dog uses his olfactory system intensively for a long time. In doing so, it is especially the muscles at the lower part of the neck that are stressed. Since muscle groups that are used over a long period of time tend to cramp or harden, the handler must always examine them as a precaution, even in a trained tracking dog.

Intensive search with slightly wagging tail.

Horizonal tail position during focused tracking.

Stress Impact of the Collar and Harness

In addition to the dog's posture, the attachment and pull of the leash can affect the dog when tracking. Depending on how the leash is attached, the effects are slightly different as can be seen in the photos on the following two pages. With a tracking harness, the leash attachment is above the back. This means that part of the spine directly under the carabiner is, or may be, stressed. This can happen even if the carabiner is not resting on the spine. It is possible that shoulder mobility is limited.

If the leash is attached to the collar or the Böttger harness, the dog's head tends to be pulled down and back when tracking. This especially stresses the upper part of the neck muscles.

Attachment of the leash directly to the collar. This causes a downward pull backward at the neck and shoulders.

Attachment of the leash to the harness. This causes a upwward pull at the neck and shoulders.

Other Effects of Tracking Work on the Dog's Body May Include:

- Increased body temperature of the dog due to increased effort.

- Decrease of focus.

- Dog fatigue.

- A strain on the nasal mucosa, which is normally slightly moisturized. Especially in a dry and hot air temperature, the nasal mucosa dries out quickly and becomes more prone to irritation. When the ground is very dry and dusty, the dog picks up small dust particles when sniffing, which become lodged in the nose. The dog then tries to clear the dust particles from the nasal passage by sneezing, sometimes also by rubbing with the paw.

- Stings/bites by insects (especially when eating infested food).

Severe Stresses:

- Tracking in very hot conditions (danger of overheating and dehydration)
- Tracking very long and difficult tracks if the dog is in poor physical condition
- Tracking under strong psychological pressure
- Strong persistent pulling while tracking

All these situations should be avoided.

Warm-up and Stretching Exercises

Before tracking training, the muscles of the tracking dog should be well supplied with blood and ready for action. Allow your dog some warm-up training. Its duration depends on several factors, including the outside temperature, and should also be adapted to the individual dog. Training according to the motto "Get out of the car and onto the track" promotes tension and injuries. Exercises in which the dog actively moves are very suitable for warming up. Stretching exercises, where the position is held for a few seconds, are not recommended for warming up. The following exercises are only representative of the large number of useful warm-up exercises. For the exercises described and others, consult a dog physical therapist who can also show you exercises specifically tailored to your dog.

1. Warm up trunk muscles and neck muscles.

- Dog runs a figure eight around the legs.
- Dog runs in front of the handler doing tight turns.

Stretching the long back muscles as the dog runs a figure eight.

2. Stretching the shoulder and elbow muscles.

With a "high paw" the dog stretches his elbow and shoulder muscles.

3. Stretching the long back muscles as the dog runs a figure eight.

- Put your dog in the dancing position (not suitable for restless and very impulsive dogs).

- After the workout, have your dog do stretching exercises to loosen tense muscles. Dog sits in front of and, if facing the handler, with the handler's legs to the right and left of the dog's torso. Slowly guide the dog's head straight up with treats. Before the dog shows evasive movements, stop and guide the head back down with food between his front legs.

The dog runs in front of the handler making tight circles in both directions.

4. General information about stretching exercises.

- Hold stretching positions for about 5 seconds, always with one hand on the dog. This gives him security. Perform all movements very slowly, do not work against the dog's resistance, and if the dog avoids the intended movement, immediately stop the movement.

- To loosen the muscles, you can also massage your dog. To do this, he sits in front of you with his back to you. Gently stroke down to the right and left NEXT to the spine in a spiral motion. Start at the base of the neck and work your way down to the base of the tail. Similarly, you can gently massage the hardened muscle cords of the lower neck. Again, it makes sense to have a dog physical therapist show you the exact procedure.

Stretching the front and back neck muscles.

Physiotherapy for Tracking Dogs
- an Interview with Mirjam Knauer

Mirjam Knauer is a physiotherapist for both humans and dogs; she specializes in sports- and service dogs. Not only does she have two different practices for dog physiotherapy but she also offers seminars in various countries including in Latvia, Germany, and Switzerland.

Mirjam Knauer, state-certified physiotherapist.

What are the most common problems that occur in your physiotherapy practice with tracking dogs?

Mirjam Knauer: Most often, dog owners report that their dog has poor endurance, which they notice while tracking. Since this is related to cardio-respiratory processing, it makes sense to conduct a thorough conditioning training program to complement tracking training. This could improve tracking work. It is also very common to find problems with the elbow joints due to the increased pressure load as well as cervical spine problems.

What causes them?

Mirjam Knauer: In general, this is difficult to answer. Most often they are caused by lack of knowledge of the owners, because many still give little thought or understanding to holistic training. Among other things, tracking work causes compression on the joint cartilage. This compression should be reduced by appropriate measures, including massage.

Stretching all the back muscles and upper neck muscles (difficult but effective).

What is particularly dear to your heart with regard to the health of tracking dogs?

Mirjam Knauer: Tracking is often dismissed as not really being strenuous for the dog's body. But it is. That's why it's important to prepare the dog physically for the upcoming stress. This could be done through balance exercises, massage of the stressed muscles, endurance training or agility exercises.

What could a warm-up to prevent injuries look like?

Mirjam Knauer: The dog needs to be taken from the car right before tracking, let him move, and do agility exercises with the dog. Appropriate exercises are, for example, give a high paw, bowing, and have the dog turn his head to the right and to the left.

With a "high paw" you stretch the elbow and neck muscles.

Recognizing Health Problems

During tracking work, health problems not exhibited prior to tracking can become apparent due to the various strains on the dog's body. Not every warning sign such as a missed cue or incorrect response can be explained by training mistakes or a demotivation of the dog. Here are just a few examples:

Warning Sign	Possible Health Problems
Oblique indicating	Pain when lying down
Inexplicable problems at corners	Impairment in the respiratory tract (e.g., rhinitis)
Slow or hesitant circling before lying down when indicating	Inflammation of the testicles, pain in the musculoskeletal system, female dog in heat, abdominal pain, etc.
Declining motivation	Pain of any kind
Sudden multiple stops on the track	Pain in the musculoskeletal system, abdominal pain, pain in the spine, pain during breathing
Unexplained unusual breathing sound	Disease in the area of the respiratory tract
Unexplained anxiety or panic symptoms	Indication of, among other things, Lyme disease or anaplasmosis which is a bacterial tickborne disease

Note that the behavior of a dog during the tracking work is sometimes also a reflection of the state of mind of the handler. Excitement, stress, demotivation or inattention of the handler are sometimes mirrored by the dog and show themselves in a corresponding manner.

Agricultural tracking terrain: forage field and a field with emerging crops. This may be an indication of pesticides being applied.

Health Hazards in the Tracking Area (Pesticides, Fertilizers...)

During tracking work, odor particles are intensively inhaled when breathing. And because the tracking dog has his nose close to the ground, he picks up particles particularly close to the ground. These can be relatively harmless dust particles or flower pollen, but also can be pesticides and fertilizers. Therefore, you should not exercise on fields that have been treated with artificial fertilizers or pesticides, or only with a greater time interval between practices. Some meadows are treated with herbicides. Fresh tractor tracks can be an indicator of that. Furthermore, toxic bait is often put in mice holes to reduce excessive population. It is best to wait until it has rained and the unhealthy substances have seeped deeper into the soil. Fresh slurry or manure in the field is usually less dangerous for the dog, but still not recommended. The ammonia smell is very unpleasant for the dog and irritates the nasal mucous membranes. Additionally, both the handler and the dog will pick up an unpleasant odor. Even more problematic is a terrain where sewage sludge has been spread. Studies have shown that this sludge contains dangerous bacteria, which the dog may inhale during tracking work.

Legal Considerations

The area where the dog handler trains his tracking dog is usually an agricultural area and private property. In Germany, everyone has the right to recreate in the great outdoors. Even entering fields and meadows is generally allowed. However, you may only enter meadows and fields during the time when they are not being used for agricultural purposes. A field may not be entered between sowing and harvesting and a meadow may not be entered between the end of March and the end of October/ November in Germany.

If possible, the dog handler should train with his dog all year round. In order to do so, he absolutely needs the permission of the respective farmer, owner or any user of the terrain. If the dog handler obtains this consent, he will save himself a lot of trouble. He should describe to the farmer or owner exactly how a tracking training runs and that neither the dog handler nor his dog will damage the area.

2. Training Know How

How to get the Dog to Love Tracking

A dog focused on his handler is the most important prerequisite for successful training.

Successful dog training requires the dog's attention because how can the dog learn anything if he doesn't pay attention to what his handler does or says? The practice often looks different. The dog is interested in everything: other dogs, a cat, the car driving away, etc. and the handler stands by and does not know how to get the attention of his dog.

But without attention there is no communication. Without communication there is no motivation. Without motivation there is no learning. And without learning there is no successful training. This is true in all dog sports, including tracking. Therefore, in this chapter you will find the basics of modern dog training, as well as proven training methods combined with the findings of behavioral research on dogs. If you apply these training principles, your dog will learn in a structured way that is adapted to his learning style. You can communicate successfully with him and build up the training so that your dog is neither under- nor overchallenged.

Training a dog is not easy. We have the fundamental problem that we cannot make ourselves understood by our dogs through language. This means: **A dog does not understand our language with its sentences and contexts. He cannot learn via insight.**

He can learn to associate individual words with a meaning, but the handler should never forget that a dog cannot understand language in the human sense. We cannot explain an exercise to him. Neither can he understand phrases like, "If you don't do this now, you'll be put on a leash." At best, he has learned to interpret the change in tone as a warning sign.

Life-Long Learning

You need to adapt the way you teach your dog to his capabilities. Dogs want to learn new things and are able to do so as long as we are open to understanding their way of communication and learning. Learning serves survival. Therefore, dogs and humans learn throughout their lives. They learn how to best get food, how to behave in the pack and much more. The goal is mostly to improve the dog's own state. For the dog, it is about satisfying his needs (e.g., hunger, reproduction, etc.) and avoiding harm. Besides learning survival skills, there is learning which is often triggered by curiosity. This learning improves the dogs' adaptation to their environment. And dogs always learn through observation, even if we do not always intend that.

Which learning processes can we use for training? From the abundance of possibilities, here are the most important ones, first in bullet points.

A dog learns:

- By the consequences of his behavior (operant conditioning)
- By associating a stimulus with an unconscious response (classical conditioning)
- Through habituation
- By increasing the response to a stimulus (sensitization)
- Through play
- In social interaction
- When a reaction fails to occur (extinction)
- In connection with the respective situation, context-related
- Continually

And these learning processes succeed best:

- With good motivation and positive reinforcement
- With a suitable expectation of the dog (not too low and not too high)
- In small learning steps
- Through many repetitions
- Through consistent consequences (praise or reprimand)
- With an understandable communication between dog and handler
- By generalizing what has been learned
- In a relaxed environment (e.g., a relaxed handler)

You will find more details on these bullet points in the following chapters. They are the basis of any successful training.

Attention

Nothing works in training without attention. Both the dog and the handler must be attentive and focused during training. From an early age, the dog should learn to pay attention to his handler. But also the handler has to notice when his dog wants to get attention, for example by looking at his handler. And this is what every dog does from an early age. Even a puppy will snuggle up to the handler's legs, look at him, jump up at him, or nudge him with his snout. It is important that you notice and respond to these attempts at contact. Otherwise, your dog will give them up after just a few weeks since he was unsuccessful in getting attention. Don't let it get that far. Keep an eye on your dog. If he looks at you, show a reaction: call him to you, pet him, give him some food, praise him or just look at him. Eye contact signals to your dog that you see him and are paying attention. Attention is based on reciprocity. We can't expect attention from our dog if we ignore him. Take advantage of your dog's social skills and needs and become a team. Always check the quality of your relationship with your dog: Can you get your dog's attention? Does your dog pay attention to you when you call his name?

Motivation

Good motivation and willingness to work together by both dog handler and dog are the most important prerequisites for successful training. And this should be the case not only on the part of the dog but also the handler.

Who doesn't know dogs that like to do all kinds of things, but have no interest in doing what their handler wants them to do? What motivates a dog to do one thing and not another? What is the driving force behind his behavior?

Directed attention....

...leads to action...

...and a positively trained recall.

Self-Motivation and External Motivation

Some things a dog does on his own (self-motivation). These include behaviors that carry their reward within themselves. These are:

- Hunting
- Prey behavior
- Eating
- Social contact (playing together, doing things together, physical contact with his humans as well as his dog friends)
- Curiosity and exploration. It remains with most dogs throughout their lives
- This also includes swimming, running or herding for some dogs
- Which of these points is particularly attractive to the dog is very much dependent on the breed. He will choose the behavior that most enhances his own well-being.

Motivation can also be triggered by the dog handler (external motivation). If a dog shows the behavior desired by the handler, he is rewarded with food or praise or something similar. In training, a dog can also be motivated by learned substitute articles instead of food.

Expectation and Distraction Level

A dog's motivation can vary depending on the level of expectation and need, and it can change very quickly. For example, in one moment a dog may be motivated to follow a laid out track, in the next moment he picks up the trail of a hare and becomes highly motivated to follow it. Motivation is usually linked to the dog's state of distractibility. A very high motivation also means high distraction in many dogs.

For successful tracking training we need a constantly motivated dog who works the track and is not distracted by anything. We achieve this through appropriate training that keeps the dog's motivation in mind and, if necessary, supports and encourages it. We achieve the best motivation through positive reinforcement, not through tracking out of fear of otherwise negative

Playing promotes the human-dog relationship.

consequences for the dog. Often these dogs, trained with fear, do not show joyful tracking behavior and quickly give up when they encounter problems. The handler must ensure throughout the training that his dog's motivation to track is maintained. That is why he must be able to recognize the first signs of demotivation (e.g., increased lifting of the head or examining mouse holes next to the track). He should know what motivates his dog again and change the training accordingly. However, not only low motivation but also too high motivation reduce the learning success for the dog.

Food Motivation

Motivation via food is very well suited for tracking training. Food serves not only as a motivational object but also as a reward for a desired behavior and for training control. Most dogs, even bad eaters, are very well motivated by food. But often the handler's idea of what his dog likes and the dog's preferences do not match. You will find more details in Chapter 3, Training Structure: Step by Step which follows. If a dog cannot be motivated by food even after many attempts, other types of motivation can be used, such as playing together.

Again and again: food on the trail!

A Helpful Tip:
Observe what motivates your dog and how you can control his level of expectation. Examples of this can be found in the following table.

Motivation Type	Level of Motivation Can Be Influenced by
Food	Consistency and taste of the treats and treats size
	Feeding frequency
	Combined with digging out the food (jar method)
	Amount of food, jackpot at the end of the track
	Saturation level of the dog before track work
Toys	Type of toy and way of playing, tugging, throwing, fetching, retrieving.
	Duration of the game
	Game intensity
Social Contact	Praise
	Petting
	Expressive enthusiasm of the dog handler

Intermittent Rewards

You achieve an increase in motivation also through an intermittent or variable reward. Instead of rewarding each successful action of the dog, reward every now and again. Studies have shown that the anticipation alone is a motivator. Motivation is increased by not always rewarding the dog with the same frequency and with the same motivational object. The "maybe" of the reward increases motivation.

It is a common misconception that food or any other type of motivation is eventually no longer necessary on the track. If the motivational object is left out permanently, in most cases the dog will slowly start to lose motivation. If the handler notices this very late, it is usually difficult to motivate the dog to track intensively again. It is important to recognize the first signs of unmotivated tracking and to react appropriately in training. Of course, the frequency of the food is slowly reduced in the long run but never completely left out.

Pay close attention to this concept. Motivation during training is the basis of successful training. Observe your dog closely and notice what motivates or demotivates your dog.

> A dog's chances to learn are the greatest if the dog is motivated, has a medium level of physical agitation, and the training must be rewarding for the dog.

Cooperation

In addition to the dog's motivation, his willingness to cooperate with his handler is also important for successful training. This willingness varies from breed to breed and from dog to dog but it can be fostered by the handler. A dog needs stable social relationships. It is up to the handler to satisfy this basic need of his dog and to cultivate the relationship with his dog from the beginning. Real bonding takes time as well as empathy and good observation skills on the part of the handler. A handler should be a reliable and attractive partner to his dog. This happens if the handler takes the leadership in the team and is engaged with his dog. He also conveys security to his dog when he reacts predictably and consistently. For example, if the handler does not want his dog to chase cats, he should consistently forbid and stop this, regardless of whether he is currently stressed, balanced or impatient.

Just the two of us, everything else is unimportant.

Communication

For training, we need a way to help our dog understand what behavior we want or don't want from him. How can he distinguish praise from reprimand? How can we communicate with our dog so that he understands us?

Non-Violent Communication

Modern dog training is characterized by successful non-violent communication between dog and handler. A dog that does what is asked of him out of fear of punishment is becoming a training practice of the past. In dog sports, training is increasingly characterized by respect for the dog and knowledge of appropriate forms of teaching for training often referred to as positive reinforcement.

At the beginning of every communication, attention of both the handler and dog is needed. Otherwise, sent signals are not perceived at all. The truism "It takes two to communicate" is also valid in dog training. The handler must pay attention to his dog and vice versa.

Communication - the transmission of information from a sender to a receiver - involves the reaction of the receiver. A person communicates a lot through language. We can exchange thoughts, convey knowledge, and discuss future and past events through it. A dog cannot do that. He does not understand the information content of our language, with far-reaching consequences for training. To recap, you cannot explain an exercise to a dog through language. You have to find other ways of communication. Dogs are excellent observers who primarily communicate through body language. That is why it is rather easy for a dog to interpret humans' body language and understand gestures. Furthermore, he can learn to put meaning to individual words and link them to a behavior. In the case of auditory signals, tone of voice and sharpness of tone also play an important role. If you want to praise your dog, for example, it is primarily important to speak in a high-pitched, friendly voice.

> A dog primarily "understands" our body language (facial expressions, posture, hand signals, etc.), our smell (fear sweat, smell of illness, etc.) and our tone of voice.

Happy anticipation of the dog.

How does the dog handler react to this?

The joyful expectation of the dog is met with open arms.

Focused?

Dogs perceive very precisely when they have our attention. They notice this beyond just direct eye contact, but also whether one's body, especially the head, is turned towards them. They also notice when we are inattentive. Studies show very clearly a connection between the attention of the dog handler and the obedience of the dog.

For example, in a tracking trial, a dog tracks very intensively for the first two legs of the trial when the track is straight lines. Suddenly, completely unexpectedly, the dog shows very unfocused behavior and clearly makes mistakes. After the trial, the handler said that he was so thrilled with his dog's track behavior on the first two legs that he then let go of his initial line tension. He thought after the first two legs that his dog "got it." Therefore, the handler's concentration and attention decreased significantly. And the dog showed the same behavior. Coincidence or correlation?

> Communicate with your dog through clear non-verbal body language. Observe your dog to see if he has understood your information. The better you can make yourself understood by your dog, the better you can adapt your training to your dog and train him successfully.

Petting is uncomfortable for the dog in this situation.

Dog style communication.

Importation communication – what does the positioning of the dogs mean?

How Dogs Express Themselves

We often don't understand what a dog is trying to communicate because he communicates with us as he would with other dogs. It is up to us to learn and understand his way of expression. A dog communicates primarily through his body language, but also through his vocalizations such as barking, squealing, growling, and the like. Unless you understand this, you may have to guess what your dog is trying to tell you. Always assume that you may misunderstand your dog. Watch your dog closely in a variety of situations. For example, does he turn his head away when you pet him? Possibly he is uncomfortable being pet on that part of his body or in that situation. Does he start licking his mouth? Possibly he is uncomfortable with our behavior and is trying to calm you as a preventive measure.

The communication of a dog with his handler is not always clear. And since it usually happens silently, the handler often does not even notice it.

Here is an example. In a puppy group, the handlers should praise their dogs. One handler strokes his dog on the head. However, the dog keeps moving his head away from the hand. The handler does not notice this. He thinks that he has praised his dog by petting him. However, the dog likely has found the petting unpleasant and is expressing this through his body's reaction. It was not until the trainer called the handler's attention to his dog's reaction that the handler observed the dog's reaction and changed his petting behavior as a result. In this case, the dog's communication was quite clear, only the handler did not notice it and thus did not understand it.

A pleasant stimulus: running, hunting...   *...playing*

Praise and Reprimands

The most common forms of communication used in training by handlers are praise or verbal reprimands. Keep in mind your dog does not understand your words but infers their meaning from the sharpness of tone, pitch and volume. Therefore, your praise must be clearly different from a reprimand, especially in pitch and sharpness of tone. Usually, praise can be expressed calmly, kindly, and with a more high pitched voice whereas a reprimand is sharper, with a deeper and more growling voice.

Praise can be expressed in different degrees: effusively, enthusiastically, normally or slightly. A gradation is also possible when reprimanding. If a dog shows an unwanted behavior while tracking, for many dogs an unwilling noise from the handler is enough for the dog to stop the unwanted behavior. However, he should then already know what is expected of him in this situation.

Example: A dog has been showing well focused tracking behavior with his nose close to the ground for a long time. He raises his head when distracted by the barking of another dog. The handler makes a noise voicing disapproval and the dog immediately lowers his head and continues his trackwork with his nose low. He should get verbal praise for that.

> If you signal to your dog early and always consistently what you want and what you don't want, small hints to your dog are usually enough for him to show the desired behavior or refrain from the unwanted behavior.

Two Examples

The trash can. If your dog keeps getting into the trash can at home and you catch him doing it, he gets reprimanded every time. If he stops what he is doing, you praise him. If he continues to rummage in the trash can, you should immediately stop him. And remember that praise or reprimand must be given within about two seconds, otherwise there is a great danger that your dog will relate it to a behavior that you are not trying to influence. It's important that your reaction is always the same even if you don't feel like reprimanding your dog at this moment. This is the only way that your dog will learn which behavior is wanted and which behavior he is supposed to refrain from. But if you tolerate his behavior once because you are just very patient today and the trash can was not very full, and only at the third time have you had enough and you react very agitated, the dog may not understand what you mean. Especially if at his next attempt to get into the trash can, you again do not react or only react with a friendly "No."

On the track. In tracking training, a dog tracks in a very unfocused manner on the first few legs. He examines several mouse holes. The handler then gives the auditory signal "No." The dog does not react. After some time the dog continues tracking. He does not take the first two corners exactly. The handler becomes increasingly angry and as his dog deviates further from the track, the auditory signals become increasingly louder and sharper. At the fourth corner, which is again not exactly followed, he scolds his dog loudly and gives a very sharp auditory signal "No" followed by a "Search." From this point on the dog tracks in a very focused manner and follows the track exactly to its end. Interpretation: The dog had learned that just the auditory signal "No" has no negative effects for him. Only when a sharp tone of voice or a greater volume is added, he must expect unpleasant reactions from the handler, such as quickly blocking the leash or stopping the training.

If the dog is to learn not to pick up anything while going for a walk, this must be consistently practiced (conditioned).

Classical Conditioning
Dogs learn by making connections (conditioning).

Example: The dog handler opens the food can in the kitchen and his dog, who was asleep before, is immdieately standing next to him. How does this happen? The dog has learned through many repetitions that he will get food as soon as he hears the sound that is made when the food can is opened. A case of classical conditioning. For the dog, a stimulus that is actually insignificant (the sound of the can being opened) takes on the significance of a previously significant stimulus (food).

Example: A dog tracks intensively along the track. The handler is 16 feet behind him. The dog masters a difficult spot with confidence. If the handler wants to praise his dog for this, he must do so within two seconds of the behavior shown. Since he cannot do this in time with food or a pet due to the distance to his dog and because this would also interrupt the training, the dog is initially only praised for his behavior by an auditory signal. This will be successful only if the dog has previously positively linked this signal outside the track with food or petting. The signal can be a praise word or something similar. It should be conditioned in such a way that the dog continues to show the behavior even after the signal. A conditioned praise word, e.g., "Great" is a well suited indirect signal to motivate the dog to continue to show a desired behavior.

Food on the track is a pleasant stimulus that rewards and reinforces the examination of footprints on the track.

Operant Conditioning

Operant conditioning occurs when a dog learns from the consequences of his behavior. The consequences can be either:

- Pleasant which motivates the dog to repeat the desired behavior
- Unpleasant which discourages the dog from repeating the behavior

It is worth taking a closer look at operant conditioning. We need it to successfully influence our dogs' behavior. Operant conditioning includes four types of reinforcers that either promotes or discourages the dog's behavior. As a consequence following the dog's behavior, the handler can:

Provide a reinforcer that is pleasant from the dog's point of view. This can be anything that is naturally motivating for the dog. They are referred to as primary reinforcers and include food, playing, running, chasing, tugging, shaking, digging, body contact. Simply put, the dog exhibits a behavior and is reinforced for it. When a wanted behavior is performed but cannot be immediately rewarded (and this happens in tracking often), a secondary reinforcer or "marker" can be applied. This includes using a clicker, praise, hand movements, and noise to let the dog know a reward will follow. These must be classically conditioned beforehand. Only then will the secondary reinforcer elicit the same positive response as the primary reinforcer to which it refers. Example: In tracking training, food is placed in the shoe prints for the dog to eat when he examines the print as desired. He will therefore continue to examine each shoe print.

Remove an unpleasant stimulus. Unpleasant does not automatically mean painful.

In tracking training, overly-motivated dogs often pull extremely hard on the leash. This is unpleasant for the dog. As soon as the dog no longer pulls so hard, he experiences a simultaneous relief in his situation and will probably change his behavior (sometimes only after some time).

Remove a pleasant stimulus. A pleasant stimulus is, for example, the handler's attention. If the dog shows an undesirable behavior, the dog is ignored for a short time. Only when he behaves as desired again, does he get attention. However, some dogs react to non-attention with aggression or they do not care as much about the handler's attention as, for example, chasing a cat. A handler should therefore use this reinforcer very judiciously and watch closely to see if removing the stimulus has the desired effect.

For well-trained tracking dogs, tracking is associated with a very positive expectation (pleasant stimulus). If the handler stops the track work because the dog did not behave as desired, this termination will be perceived by the dog as a reprimand or "punishment." It will motivate him to behave as desired by the handler during the next training session. However, the sudden termination can be very demotivating and frustrating for some dogs, causing them to lose the fun of track work. You can see from the reaction of your dog whether your measure has the desired success.

Add an unpleasant stimulus. Unpleasant stimuli include vocal reprimands, leash tugs, nudges and increasing the degree of difficulty. The relationship with the handler must in no case be damaged by an unpleasant stimulus. Therefore, observe your dog closely. Unpleasant stimuli are to be avoided in tracking training. They usually have negative effects on motivation and track behavior (avoidance behavior, evasive behavior, stress symptoms, demotivation). Sometimes this happens inadvertently. If the tracks are too difficult, a dog will make more mistakes. If the dog handler is stressed and blames his dog for the undesirable behaviors, in addition to the frustration of a too difficult track, the dog can be demotivated and no longer wants to joyfully continue tracking.

Timing
Additionally, proper timing is very important in both operant and classical conditioning. The consequence (reinforcer stimulus) to a behavior must occur within 1 to 2 seconds. The handler's full attention must therefore be with his dog so that he can react in time.

Effects on Emotions

The different reinforcer stimuli not only affect the dog's behavior, but also his emotions.

Reinforcer Stimuli and Their Consequences

	Give a Pleasant Stimulus	Remove an Unpleasant Stimulus (Something Unpleasant Is Ended)
Example	Food, play, praise, petting	Unblocking the leash, feeding a hungry dog, giving attention to an unattended dog, eliminating boredom or loneliness through training
Emotions of the Dog	Joy, affection, motivation	Relief, motivation
Desired Behavior Will Be	More likely and more intense	More likely and more intense
Risks	Over-motivation and thus inhibition of learning, distraction from the actual task	Unpleasant behavior is less important than the unwanted behavior, dog may not stop his behavior

	Give an Unpleasant Stimulus	Remove a Pleasant Stimulus (Something Pleasant Is Removed)
Example	Reprimand, leash jerk	Dog is no longer paid attention to, a pleasant activity (playing) is stopped in the event of undesirable behavior
Emotions of the Dog	Fear, pain, aversion	Demotivation
Desired Behavior Will Be	Rarer	Rarer
Risks	Dog avoids situation, strain on the relationship between dog and handler	Taking away something pleasant is more unpleasant for the dog than the internal reward of the undesirable behavior, dog may not stop his behavior

How a dog responds to each reinforcer varies greatly from individual to individual. If an unwanted quiet noise is sufficient as an unpleasant stimulus for one dog, a loud emphatic auditory signal "No" is required for another dog. While some dogs find a mild reprimand or repeated corrections so unpleasant that they are strongly demotivated and no longer want to track, other dogs can be corrected in this way without any problems. While one dog is motivated by friendly praise, another dog needs a strong emotional outburst from his handler to be motivated. Such an emotional outburst could in turn motivate another dog to undesirable behavior, such as jumping up at the handler.

Undesireable hunting behavior on the track. Where is the rabbit?

The reward used must be a reward from the dog's point of view. Not every food achieves the desired effect, and not all dogs find, for example, petting during an exercise pleasant. An intended praise thus becomes something unpleasant for the dog and makes the behavior desired by the handler less likely to happen. Observe your dog's reaction to the different reinforcers and draw the appropriate conclusions.

Common handler errors

Poor timing. A dog is tracking intensively; he is looking for every single step. The handler wants to praise him for this, but has a reaction time of 3 seconds from decision to execution. At the moment of praise, however, the dog is in the process of investigating a mouse hole, so the handler has praised an undesirable behavior. The handler can never be sure that the dog has learned exactly what he intended. It is important that the handler always takes this into account during training.

Indication errors. A tracking dog learns to indicate an article. He should lie down in front of the article, or the article could be between his paws. The dog learns quickly and after only a few repetitions it looks as if he has understood exactly what to do. During a later training session, the article is lying in a strong headwind for the first time and the dog lies down about 9 feet in front of the article. The dog smelled it early and immediately reacted by lying down. He had learned, without the handler noticing: he should lie down as soon as he smells the article. It is arduous to undo this false link and to teach the dog correct indicating behavior.

You see, false links sometimes arise unnoticed and unintentionally. The handler can only recognize them by his dog's behavior. Many, even most, of the undesirable behaviors a dog makes in training, are based on false links. Rarely is there a lack of will on the part of the dog behind incorrect track behavior!

From the multitude of possible faulty linkages during tracking training, here is a small selection:

Events	Example
Linking unintentional things by the dog	Dog should learn to track every shoe print, unintentionally he learns to track along a seed groove because the first tracks were along seed furrows. The tracks are always laid by the same person. The dog does not track foreign tracks or, if he does, he is unsure of himself.
Inconsistent reaction by the handler to his dog's repeated behavior	Investigating mouse holes is not always reprimanded because the handler is not attentive enough or is overwhelmed with his reaction. This leaves the dog unsure if searching mouse holes is allowed or not desired. He is likely to exhibit this behavior again. It is part of his exploratory behavior and is associated with pleasant emotions.
Reaction of the dog handler is too late	Dog tracks intently, is briefly distracted by a noise and raises his head. Then he continues to track intensively. The handler wants to reprimand him for lifting his head, but he does it too late, just at the moment the dog tracks intensively again.
Simultaneous events	Unpleasant events during the track like cows scaring the dog, other dogs attacking, or biting ants are associated with tracking and the dog then avoids tracking.

Strengthening desired behaviors

A dog usually learns a behavior but that may not last forever. If the desired behavior is not practiced again and again, the probability that the dog will reliably show the learned behavior will decrease. The learned behavior will be unlearned or become extinct. Depending on the type of dog, this phenomenon of extinction in training can occur very quickly or with some delay.

This is the reason why it makes sense to reward the dog again and again during track work. The motivation to track is thus stimulated and maintained again and again.

Even if it seems that a dog loves to track, it is difficult for a handler to distinguish whether it is the fun of tracking or the expectation of finding food. Experience shows that most dogs need food to maintain track motivation. See the chapter on Motivation on page 28 for more details.

This undistracted dog is ready to track!

Auditory Signals

In tracking dog training, we use auditory signals to signal our dog what behavior we want from him. These auditory signals must first be conditioned with the behaviors we want our dog to perform. In the previous chapter you have already learned about the different types of conditioning. We will apply this knowledge to concrete examples. In training, we need the auditory signal "Search" and a termination auditory signal, for example "No." The dog needs to learn the meaning of "No" in daily life. Other useful auditory signals would be "Sit," "Down" or "Stand," depending on which type of indicating articles you are teaching your dog.

How Do You Teach Your Dog the Meaning of an Auditory Signal?

The goal here is to get your dog to perform the desired behavior on his own, with the support of food or light touch. For example, to condition the auditory signal "Search," place food in the search field. As soon as the dog responds by sniffing the ground with his nose, keep saying "Search" in a friendly and motivating manner, preferably in a high pitch voice. After a lot of repetitions (about 60), the dog will connect the signal "Search" with food on the ground and find the food. He may also have already learned that food can only be found on the ground which was trodden. This ground smells different to the dog than the ground not walked on.

Only after many repetitions can you assume that when you give the auditory signal "Search," the dog will lower his nose and start searching. Even then, it is not yet clear whether he has also associated the auditory signal with the track, i.e., the changed ground scent, or initially only with the lowering of the nose and the food on the ground.

Stop Signal

In training, it is important to be able to signal to the dog that the behavior he has just shown is not desired and that he should stop it. Therefore, we need a stop signal.

Your dog should already know and follow the stop signal before the tracking training. Each dog may have his own signal that indicates "Stop." There are many gradations and types of stop signals that the handler can use. It might be a sound voicing unwillingness, a sharp "No," it might be a sharp "No" combined with a gesture, or it could be a frightening noise. The earlier and more consistently a dog learns these signals and thereupon interrupts his action, the lower the necessary influence on the dog needs to be. However, the higher the dog's state of excitement, the stronger the stop signal usually has to be. Since the dog is usually not in a high state of excitement during the track work, a sound voicing unwillingness is usually enough. It becomes problematic with behaviors that trigger a high level of excitement in the dog, such as a fleeing rabbit. Sometimes the only thing that helps here is blocking the dog's leash and waiting until the excitement has subsided. In such cases, specific training outside of tracking training is necessary, where the dog learns to interrupt a prey-catching behavior as well.

> **Stop-Auditory Signal**
> Research has shown that a stop auditory signal or a visual dismissive hand signal has a greater and more lasting effect than just positive reinforcement of the desired behavior.

Interrupting a Behavior

From the beginning, teach your dog appropriate stop signals. It is important to insist that your dog interrupts his behavior. Keep in mind here that your dog must first learn to interrupt a behavior he is comfortable with. Increase the difficulty slowly. Make sure that you always have the opportunity to interrupt your dog's undesirable behavior if the dog does not listen to the stop signal. Here, too, correct timing is especially important. If the auditory signal is given later than two seconds after the dog's unwanted action, the dog usually cannot correctly associate it with that action. However, this training must never be at the expense of your relationship. If the dog interrupts his behavior, show him immediately what behavior you want from him. If he shows the desired behavior, praise him.

A good opportunity to practice a stop signal is when playing with the dog. While playing, give the auditory signal "No" along with a dismissive gesture. Prevent the dog from continuing to play. If he interrupts the game, praise him. After a short time, give another auditory signal such as "OK" and continue playing with your dog. Begin with this training in a calmer play phase so the dog has a chance to interrupt his behavior. Then only gradually increase the difficulty.

Intensive play with the dog.

The dog handler's body posture clearly signals an interruption of the game.

After the game is interupted it continues when prompted by the handler

When Is a Stop Signal Appropriate?

It is very important to be able to judge when a stop signal is appropriate. If a dog is overwhelmed and does not find the track, i.e., moves off the track, it is usually not sensible to use a stop signal. The dog is tracking intensively, but he has just lost the track momentarily. Here it is better if the handler encourages his dog to continue tracking or helps him with pointing gestures.

Dog-to-Dog Stop Signals

Dogs among themselves also use stop signals, which can be pure threat signals (growl, stern look) or calming signals (look away, random sniffing). They serve among other things as a request to accept their own personal space to avoid conflict. Normally, stop signals among dogs do not lead to a strain of the relationship. To achieve this, the receiver of the break-off signal sends conciliatory body signals as a reaction. In the handler-dog relationship, a stop signal must also not strain the handler's relationship with his dog. Observe how your dog reacts after a stop signal. Does he stop his behavior? Is he unsure of himself and does not know what to do?

Habituation and Sensitization

Habituation is both the blessing and curse of dog training. On the one hand, habituation of a dog to stimuli is desirable. For example, the dog should not bark every time the neighbor slams the car door in front of the house. On the other hand, there are situations to which the dog should not get used (i.e., reprimands). When being reprimanded, the dog should stop the undesirable behavior.

The opposite of habituation is sensitization. Here the dog does not get used to stimuli and so reacts stronger and stronger to them. Some dogs are afraid when driving in a car. Instead of getting used to it, some react more and more strongly with fear or even panic symptoms. Sometimes this behavior starts when the handler takes the car key in his hand.

Therefore, before exposing your dog to new stimuli, consider carefully whether you want him to become so accustomed to these stimuli that he no longer shows any reaction, or whether he should become increasingly sensitive to them.

Relaxed driving and staying in the car.

Habituation to distractions near the track.

Habituation and Sensitization in Tracking Training

In tracking training, we need both mechanisms. No reaction on the part of the tracking dog is desired in the following situations, among others: talking and laughing people during the tracking work, barking dogs off the track, birds flying up, crossing game tracks, cows, horses, wind turbines, long waiting times in the car, or a tangled leash.

However, a tracking dog should be sensitive, for example, to changes in the scent of the track, to praise or reprimand of the handler, to changes in the direction of the track, to articles on the track, etc.

How do you achieve habituation to environmental influences without sensitization taking place? The new stimulus, like a loud noise, should not occur too strongly at the beginning of habituation. Only when it is certain that no sensitization in the form of fear behavior or an increased reaction to the stimulus occurs, can the stimulus be intensified.

On the track, the dog should not react to talking people. First, train in an environment where people are farther away. Make it clear to your dog that you do not want your dog to react to them. If the dog shows no reaction to distant people during training, decrease the distance. Slowly increase the volume of the people talking as well. Finally, people should be able to clap their hands or laugh loudly without the dog showing any reaction.

A dog needs to be desensitized to wind turbines, other people and dogs in the tracking area.

Impulse Control

In tracking work, it is important that the dog does not follow every impulse to do something else. Depending on the breed and the dog's personality, the stimulus threshold to follow an impulse differs widely. Even a mouse running away can trigger intense prey catching behavior in a hunting dog. Here it makes sense to generally carry out training for impulse control. The dog learns to not follow every impulse immediately. He learns to control himself. Exercises where the dog has to wait are very helpful here. However, the following also applies here: increase the degree of difficulty only slowly. The dog must have the opportunity to learn to control himself. It is best to practice this with your dog over and over again outside of tracking training, increasing the difficulty slowly, and not demanding too much self-control at once.

Impulse control training example: Go to the dog's feeding place with the food bowl. Before your dog is allowed to eat, he should wait for an appropriate signal from you. You can make this clear to him both by an appropriate dismissive hand movement and by saying "No." After a short time, give him permission to eat. Slowly increase the difficulty of the exercise sessions and be creative in the design of the exercises. It is fascinating to see how a dog, after successful impulse training, holds a meat sausage in his mouth and eats it only after being told to do so by his handler. The goal of impulse training is a dog that can respond to outside stimuli in a more controlled manner.

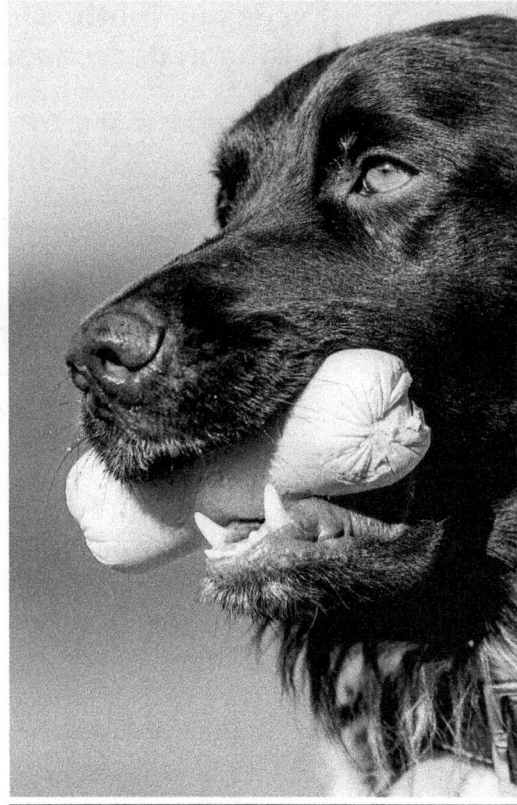

The high art of impulse control – the dog eats the sausage only when signaled to do so by his handler.

Stress While Learning

Severe stress is poison for successful learning. Mild stress, on the other hand, can lead to an increase in memory performance. But what is stress? How does it manifest itself in dogs? Stress is first of all a reaction of the body to a stimulus. Through a release of adrenaline, noradrenaline, cortisone and cortisol, the body is put into maximum readiness to perform. It can react quickly to the stimulus. The downside, however, is a reduced ability to learn the greater the stress. In extreme cases, even already learned behaviors can no longer be performed correctly. The extent to which a stimulus can trigger stress in a dog varies greatly from individual to individual. The New Year's Eve celebrations, for example, can lead to real panic attacks in some dogs while other dogs do not react to it. Additional factors in how strongly a stimulus is perceived as stress by the dog include his breed, level of training, previous experience, state of health, and relationship to the handler.

Excessive motivation can also cause stress in a dog, resulting in decreased learning ability.

In tracking training, we need a medium level of excitement. The training should not cause excessive stress in the dog (e.g., by constant overtraining, punishment or similar). A dog should learn to deal with stressful situations through a targeted, slowly increasing training.

> **Signs of Stress**
> Stress in a dog shows through panting, setting back ears, yawning, shaking himself, barking or whimpering.

Stress-Producing Moments

There are always stress-producing moments in tracking training even without any action from us. Here are a few examples:

- A dog does not find the track.
- A dog is reprimanded or corrected by the handler.
- A dog gets into a conflict between what the handler wants and what he wants himself (e.g., chasing fleeing game while doing track work).
- A handler is angry or stressed (e.g., after trouble at work, or time pressure during training). This will project on the dog.
- Indicating articles puts some dogs under stress because they actually want to keep tracking.
- It is a trial situation (e.g., barking dogs, nervous handler, other people doing track work).
- A track is too difficult for the dog's level of training.

If strong stress (e.g., threat) affects the dog, he has four possible ways to react:

- Fight, Action (Fight)
- Solidification, Freezing (Freeze)
- Avoid, Escape (Flight)
- Appease (Flirt)

None of these possible reactions support optimal learning behavior. If a dog exhibits any of these behaviors, the handler can assume that his dog is currently under severe stress.

Emotions and Learning

Both a dog and a handler learn and train more successfully when the training is associated with positive emotions such as fun and joy. Since a dog can sense the emotions of his handler, it is important that the handler also enjoys the tracking training. Otherwise, the displeasure of the handler is easily transferred to the dog. A dog handler should therefore avoid aversion, irritability, time pressure and stress during training and, if necessary, move the training to another day.

Here the guiding principle of tracking training under the aspect of emotions during learning is important: plan the training so that the dog can work the track for the most part as error-free as possible. Constant overtaxing, corrections, and failures are neither motivating for the dog nor for the handler. They lead to negative emotions and thus to an impaired learning behavior of the dog.

Physical and Mental Fitness

For tracking work the dog needs to be in good physical and mental condition. Nose work stresses the entire organism. Both the circulatory and the musculoskeletal systems are strained. Therefore, a general conditioning regimen (cycling, jogging, etc.) adapted to the age of the dog can be helpful for general fitness. In addition, the dog must track focused during the entire time he is working. This requires a high level concentration conditioning, which must be slowly built up in training. For the dog handler it is important to be able to recognize the fatigue symptoms of his dog. These vary from dog to dog. Signs of fatigue can be:

- A strong lifting of the head. A slight lifting of the nose is usually an attempt to relax, which does not necessarily signal fatigue

- A greater lowering of the tail as the tracking work progresses (note: for some dogs, lowering the tail is the working posture)

- An abrupt stop on the track

- Stopping the track work

However, all these signs can also be indicators of other problems, especially a lack of motivation on the track. Therefore, the handler must first consider the entire situation (weather, length already tracked, etc.). Then he should determine the most probable reason for the behavior shown, react appropriately, and finally check that his interpretation about the reasons for the behavior is correct.

At the first symptoms of exhaustion, the track should be stopped in a planned manner, preferably at the next article. Or quickly place a larger chunk of food on the track, unnoticed by the dog, and then end the track. Plan the next track to be correspondingly shorter.

For the necessary conditioning and concentration building, there are different strategies depending on the type of dog. Some dogs can be motivated to track somewhat shorter tracks several times a week and in between also somewhat longer ones. Other dogs, on the other hand, lose their motivation with this approach. Always pay attention to your dog's body language. Is he motivated to work the track or not? If you can only train once a week due to your dog's disposition then slowly increase the length of the tracks and do some general conditioning training outside of the track.

General fitness training is a good supplement to track training.

Training Know How Summary

- Motivate your dog to do track work. The excitement level should neither be too low nor too high.

- Keep up the motivation.

- Pay attention to the health of your dog. Offer him water before and after training. Give him a chance to relieve himself before training. Walk him before and after training.

- Build warm-up exercises and post-exercise cool-down exercises into the training routine (ritual design).

- Pay attention to a functioning communication between your dog and you. Can your dog distinguish between praise and reprimand?

- Watch your dog closely at every stage of training. Get to know your dog's body language.

- Use the different reinforcers in conditioning in a targeted and deliberate way. Learning by success is a very good reinforcer. Avoid very unpleasant experiences for the dog during training.

- If you want to correct or praise your dog, do it within 1 to 2 seconds.

- You must be aware of your dog's desired behavior throughout the entire training.

- If your dog shows an undesirable behavior, first assume that you did not train the dog correctly.

- Give correction signals only if you have the possibility to intervene in the situation (e.g., by a short leash).

- You should know the wind direction when laying the training and evaluating the training track.

- The dog should usually be able to work a training track consistently without any problems. Plan small learning steps, a slow increase in difficulty and consistent behavior of the handler (always the same reactions to the same actions of the dog).

- Review your interpretations about the reasons for your dog's unwanted behavior on the trail.

- Do not always train alone with your dog.

- Once in a while, let your dog work tracks laid by other people as well.

- Also use articles of another person.

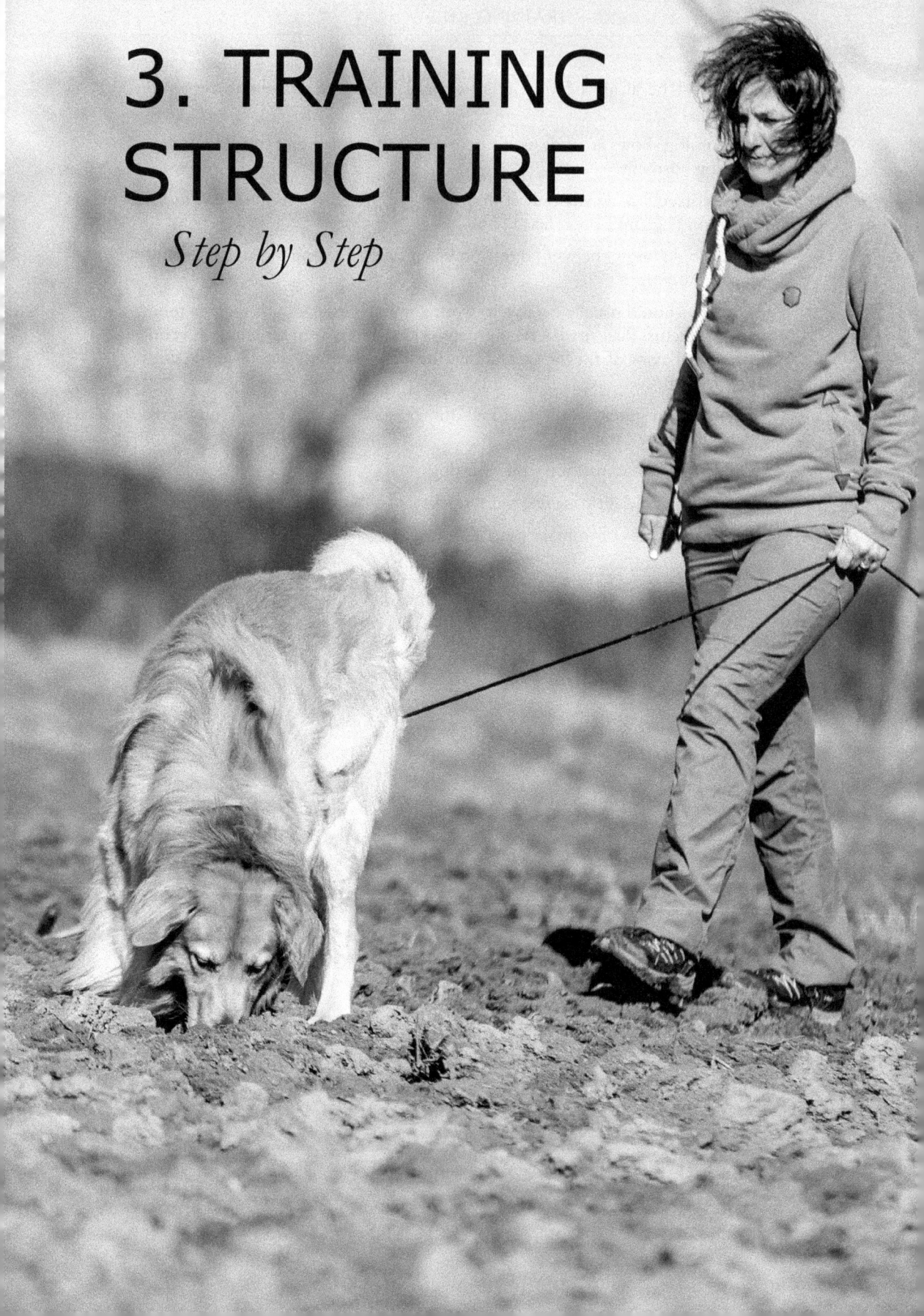

3. TRAINING STRUCTURE

Step by Step

Tracking Training Overview

Now you are almost at the beginning of actual tracking dog training. Just a few words about the general structure of the training. This includes the goals of the tracking training as well as the technical terms and then it's time for the concrete preparations of the training. For a successful training structure we should always have the goals of the training in mind, that is, a dog that tracks a trodden track unperturbed by external influences, independently solves challenges, has his nose close to the ground while doing so, and also finds the articles that are on the track and indicates them to the handler.

The Goals of Tracking Training

Even though a dog orients himself mostly by scent, finding a trodden track (one that has been laid out) is not innate to a dog. A trodden track does not normally lead to food, and therefore does not motivate a

The dog should follow the track exactly with a deep nose.

dog to search for it. Additionally, tracking is not only about finding the track, but also about how he works the track. The desired ideal track behavior is dictated by International Utility Dogs Regulations (in 2019, the IGP).

Whether you teach your dog tracking simply for fun, or whether you want to compete, in any case you will find in this book the appropriate approach to training. Of course, there are also natural talents among dogs that show the desired track behavior on their own, but these tend to be the exceptions. For all others, the following applies:

A tracking dog must learn the desired behavior. He learns it through the handler and through the training tracks (i.e., the person who lays the track). Throughout this book, the handler is assumed to be both the trainer and the track layer. Often an inexperienced handler does not yet have the experience and skills to lay a training track optimally or to give his dog the necessary support and correction during the track work. This is where the guidance of an experienced dog trainer or track layer is a great help. Also, with the help of this book, you can systematically acquire the knowledge for successful tracking training and then put it into practice.

> In training, the following training steps have proven to be successful: Training planning, execution, observation, evaluation, training adaptation.

First of all, it is important to get to know the individual learning steps and thus the training structure. After that, however, you should closely observe the dog in training and analyze his behavior. Does his behavior correspond to the desired track behavior? If not, what could be the reasons and how could you change the training so that the dog shows the desired behavior? You will find an overview of the possible reasons for a displayed undesirable behavior of the dog in training in the chapter on troubleshooting as well as sensible correction possibilities. With this background knowledge and the targeted approach to training, you can adapt the training to your dog, his abilities, dispositions and personal characteristics. What is suitable for one dog as a training track or training method may not be suitable for another. The accompanying figure shows the proven approach.

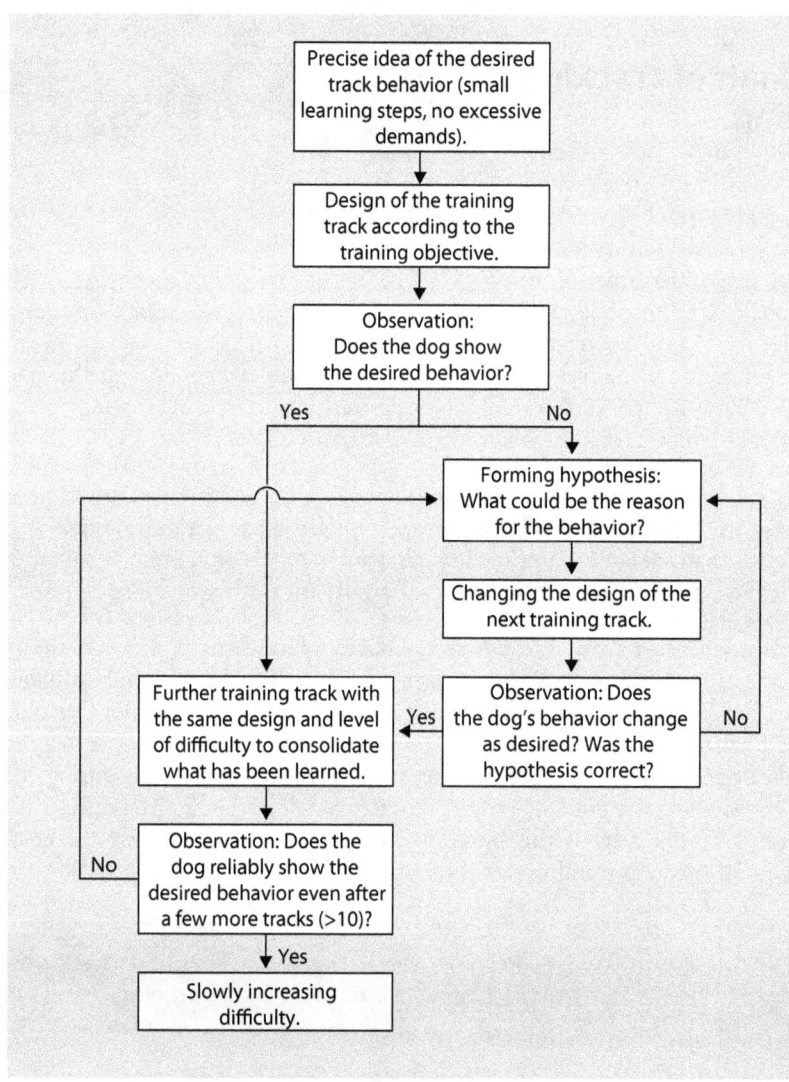

Process of successful training planning.

Therefore, in the description of the exercises covered below you will find a short summary of the exercise as well as:

- A detailed description of the exercise
- An exact description of the ideal behavior of the dog
- A brief list of foreseeable undesirable behaviors (more detailed guidance on possible corrections can be found in the appropriate chapter)
- Different levels of difficulty of the exercise
- What you as a dog handler should learn during the exercise
- A case study where you can apply your knowledge

Mostly Error-Free Learning

The difficulties of the training track are planned for the dog in such a way that he can track mostly error-free without help. In this way, the dog learns from the beginning confident consistent track behavior, self-confidence, and the ability to solve problems independently. The handler then does not have to constantly correct because his dog shows the desired track behavior. For this to succeed, predictable distractions for the dog should be avoided, especially at the beginning of training. If the dog is frequently overwhelmed while tracking, he will quickly become demotivated or restless and will become accustomed to faulty track behavior.

For a good training setup, you should be able to assess what your dog can easily learn and how you can slowly increase the demands on his track behavior. And the most important thing in any training: **You must know the exact course of the training track during training.** Only then can you judge whether your dog is tracking accurately. You will find help for laying and finding the training track in the chapter on the training track (pp. 117).

What Your Dogs Needs to Learn for Tracking Training

Here is an overview of the most important learning concepts for your dog, which will be described in detail in the next chapters. These are the requirements of the highest trial level for a competing tracking dog. These can and should be trained from the beginning according to the training level of the dog. Always following the rule: the training builds up from easy to more complex situations.

The most important steps to learn for a tracking dog:

- General track behavior and track speed
- Starting point (beginning of the track), scent pad
- Tracking a leg with road crossings and terrain changes
- Tracking a corner (acute corners and right corners)
- Tracking a semicircle
- Indicating articles

- Ignore cross track (this point is not necessary for the tracking sub-trials of IGP-1 to IGP-3)
- Condition building
- Problem solving behavior
- And all this in any weather

Technical Terms

The trial regulations have a special technical vocabulary that you should know. Here are some terms shown in the following graphic with their assignment to the sections of a track. You will find further explanations of terms in the glossary at the end of the book.

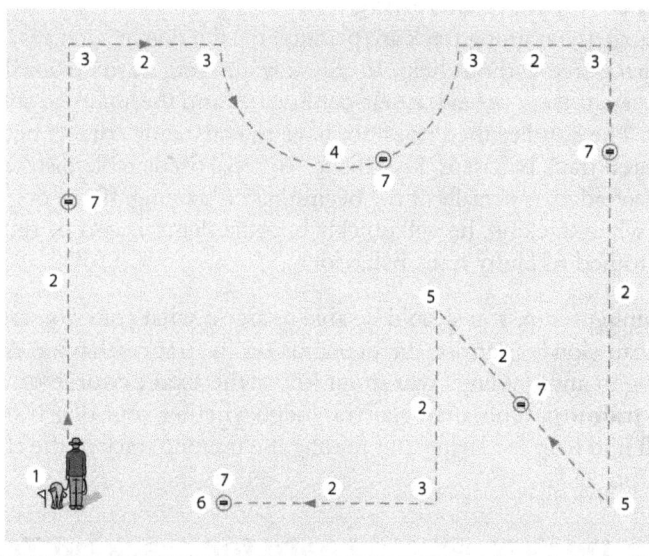

1 – Start marked with a track marker.

2 – Leg connection between two corners

3 – Corner with 90-degree angles right and left

4 – Semicircle begins and ends with a 90-dgegree angle.

5 – Acute corner (<90-degrees)

6 - End of the track

7 – Article

Equipment, Food, Terrain

Attaching the leash directly to the collar. It is passed under a foreleg, possibly the hindleg.

Equipment

Basic Equipment

You will need:

- A collar (during trial the collar used must be one that distributes the pull of the leash evenly across the neck.

- Possibly a tracking harness for a smaller dog.

- A leash (10 m long/32 feet, initially also shorter approx. 6 m/19 ½ feet, without buckles), prefer-ably made of a material that does not absorb water (e.g., Biotane), so that the leash does not become heavier when wet. Especially for small dogs, the leash should be as light as possible even when dry. It must be made of a material that can be held securely in the hand even when the dog is pulling strongly.

- Suitable treats (see p. 65)

Leashes, collars, harnesses

For tracking training, you will need a leash without buckles with a carabiner, possibly a tracking harness, food, and a terrain where you may lay a training track. For large dogs, the leash is usually attached to the collar, passed down and back between the front legs. For a small dog, it is recommended to attach the leash to a tracking harness, which must allow unobstructed breathing in the dog when he tracks with his nose close to the ground.

With or Without Leash

A dog can track with or without a leash, as well as with or without a harness. Almost all handlers prefer tracking with a leash because they can more easily see and feel changes in the dog's behavior through the leash and give the dog security by lightly pulling back on the leash. Furthermore, the handler can control his dog through the leash and correct his dog better in training in case of an undesirable behavior (blocking, braking, etc.).

Track work without a leash is possible but usually not recommended. It only makes sense for very sensitive dogs that react to the pull of the leash with avoidance behavior. Also, during the track, the leash can get caught on plants or lumps of earth in the terrain which causes a yank on the dog. Sensitive dogs get irritated, and this interrupts their tracking work.

During a trial, both tracking on a 10m (32 feet) leash and tracking without a leash are allowed. However, the handler must keep a distance of 10m (32 feet) from his dog. It depends on the dog whether or not a leash is useful. Each has its own advantages and disadvantages.

Attachment of the Leash to the Collar

In large dogs, the leash is often attached to the collar, pulled under a front leg, and passed either between the hind legs to the rear or laterally next to the corresponding hind leg. Each leash exerts a slight pull on the collar by its own weight, which slightly pulls the dog's head down. The downward pull of the leash supports the desired head position of the dog because he should track with a low nose. On the other hand, this pull stresses the cervical spine because the stronger the dog pulls on the leash the stronger the pull is. With a wide collar, this pull is distributed over a larger area on the cervical spine. On the other hand, the collar should only be as wide to not restrict the mobility of the cervical spine and hinder breathing.

Tracking with a tracking harness.

If the leash is led backwards to the side next to the hind legs, it lifts the dog's front leg upwards when the dog pulls strongly, which is uncomfortable for the dog. After some time, he then stops the hasty search and slows down. If the leash is led sideways to the rear, the dog may make an evasive movement, which is undesirable. He then runs with his body diagonally to the track. When the leash is passed backwards between the hind legs, it touches a very sensitive area on the inside of the hind legs. Sometimes this results in rubbing against the dogs' private parts. This can also be very uncomfortable. As a result, sensitive dogs will stop tracking unless they are highly motivated.

For small dogs, this attachment of the leash is hardly suitable. They easily climb over the leash, and it then runs directly from the collar to the handler and every pull on the leash pulls the dog's head up, which is undesirable. So many handlers use a tracking harness for small dogs.

Attachment of the Leash to the Tracking Harness

Attaching the leash to a tracking harness is especially suitable for small dogs because the leash does not easily get caught in the terrain. The leash is attached to the harness above the back. With this type of attachment, there is no pressure on the cervical spine. On the other hand, the spine is strained below the attachment carabiner. And this is the case even if the carabiner does not rest directly on it. Depending on the type of harness, the mobility of the shoulders may be restricted. One advantage of attaching to a tracking harness is that the line is less likely to snag on higher plant parts during the track than with other attachment methods. However, you cannot hinder a strongly pulling dog as easily.

Attaching the leash to a collar.

Tracking with harness.

A tracking harness should fit optimally. When the dog has his nose on the ground, the harness must not hinder breathing in any way or restrict free movement of the shoulder even when pulling.

Fastening to the Böttger Tracking Harness

As shown above, this tracking harness is attached to the collar. The effect on the cervical spine is therefore the same as when the carabiner is attached directly to the collar. There is a downward pull on the collar, which in turn acts on the cervical spine. The leash is passed backwards between the hind legs. The Böttger tracking harness must be well fitted. The rear strap must not extend beyond the dog's last rib. It must not constrict any soft tissues. The leash is attached to the harness below the dog. This makes it easier for it to get caught on higher plant parts.

If you use a tracking harness, you should use it exclusively for tracking work. If it is put on the dog, this dog should associate tracking work with it.

Attachment of a Second Leash to the Collar

Especially at the beginning of training, some handlers use two leashes attached to the collar. Both are led between the front legs to the rear, whereby one is led to the right of and the other to the left of the respective rear leg. One leash is the track leash and the other one is the correction leash. Both leashes can support the dog to track and allow the dog to move ahead to indicate articles. However, the handling of the two leashes is quite difficult and error-prone.

Other Useful Training Equipment

- **A starting point marker.** A stick, to mark the beginning of the track.

- **Suitable articles.** These should be made of different materials. Their color should not differ significantly from the color of the terrain. In reality, you can also find clearly visible articles at trials. The prescribed dimensions can be found in the trial regulations.

- **Rain boots or suitable sturdy boots.** Especially for wet weather or loamy ground.

- **Tracking diary or scratch paper.** For training planning and orientation when laying the track.

- **Aids for retrieving the training track (tracking chalk, etc.).** For more details, see the chapter on the training track.

- **And of course you need a motivated dog that likes to do things with you.** Without good motivation, the training will not be very successful. Observe your dog. How can you tell that your dog is ready for training? He should be healthy and not too full.

Especially with dog breeds that have not been bred to work with the handler, it is particularly important to pay attention to the dog's motivation. It must be neither too high nor too low. In both cases, the dog will not learn optimally. If

Track sketch with terrain markers.

With this equipment you can get started.

you have doubts about your dog's motivation, you will find helpful information in the chapter Training Know How (see page 28).

Training Food/Treats

Generally, we reward the dog in training with different things when he shows the desired behavior. This can be pieces of food, petting, praise, play or the like. Food, especially, has a great importance in tracking dog training.

> ### The right food characteristics
> For training, you need food that the dog swallows without chewing, that he likes to eat very much and that preferably does not stand out from the subsoil.

The Dog Determines What Food is a Reward for Him

Especially at the beginning of the training and when problems arise, the dog must be strongly motivated by the food. He must really like the food.

Finding the Favorite Food

If your dog does not show intense tracking from the beginning, first consider the choice of food. Our dogs often have different taste preferences than we think. Experiment with different foods. It is amazing how informative the "food paradise" is for this.

Set up a "Food paradise:" On a level area (e.g., asphalted path), small food piles with different food are placed at a distance of approx. 30 cm/1 foot. This can be dry food, small pieces of meat, sausages, and much more. Everything is cut to approximately the same size so that the dog can pick it up quickly. Lead your dog past the food piles

A "food paradise" for tracking dogs.   *First the dog is allowed to smell the food, and then later may eat it without a leash.*

on a leash so he can smell them but not eat them. Do not give any sound signals, such as "No" or "Leave it." Then lead your dog away a little bit and let him off the leash. Watch carefully how he behaves. He may immediately run to a particular pile and eat it completely. He will investigate other piles and eat parts but also leave parts. Some foods he may ignore altogether. You can see very quickly which food your dog particularly likes and what your dog's ranking is of favorite foods. In training, you need food with different degrees of popularity for your dog, including high value treats.

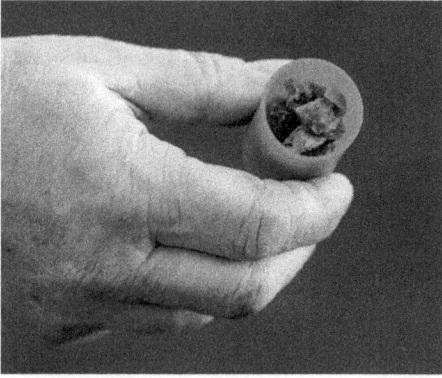

Filled food container.

Push the filled container into the track.

The dog finds the food container and digs it out enthusiastically.

It is always surprising to see in which order and how a dog eats the food laid out: does he eat everything of one type straight away or does he turn to the next type of food after just a few pieces? Many predictions of dog handlers on how their dog will behave, prove to be wrong in this experiment. For example, during training, a dog is rewarded with cheese on the track. Then he is to learn to lie down at articles that have been laid out. He does this very slowly and only with the help of pointing gestures and auditory signals. To make lying down more attractive, he is rewarded with liver sausage. His hesitant behavior still does not change, even after many weeks. Following a sudden impulse, the handler gives the dog the opportunity to choose between cheese and liver sausage outside the track. The result is surprising and is repeated with changing arrangements of cheese and liver sausage. The result does not change. The dog clearly likes cheese more than liver sausage. From the dog's point of view, the reward for tracking with cheese is much more attractive than the reward at the articles with the liver sausage. As a result, the food on the track is changed and indicating the articles is rewarded with cheese.

Different Functions of Food

Food has different functions in tracking training and thus different effects.

1. Food as a Reward for Demonstrated Behavior

The food should be easy for the dog to find and eat on the track. That way it distracts the dog less from tracking. The dog should be able to eat the food without chewing to avoid him lifting his head while chewing. The food is preferably in the shoe print, to reward tracking the step immediately. A gradation in the reward should be possible by choosing different food.

2. Food for Direct Control of Behavior

The dog should perceive the food, eat it and thereby show a certain behavior. The food must be easy or harder to find, depending on the desired behavior. For example, if a dog shows superficial tracking, food that is pressed into the shoe print (harder to find) may cause the dog to track more intensively. If a dog is to learn to ignore cross tracks, food can be placed immediately after the cross track (easy to find) at the first cross tracks in the headwind, which will encourage the dog to continue tracking and not switch to the cross track.

3. Food to Increase the Dog's Arousal Level

Food can also be used to promote motivation during tracking work. For this, the food must be particularly tasty for the dog so that his attention is focused on eating and possibly finding the food on the track. By burying food (e.g., in a small can), which the dog is allowed to dig out, the dog can get on a higher arousal or motivation level and continue tracking more motivated. However, this only works if he likes to dig up things. Put his favorite food in small plastic containers. These are sunk into the ground. At first, the lid remains open so that the dog can easily smell the contents. The dog is allowed to dig out the can and is praised for it. If he masters this after several repeats, the lid is closed, with holes in the lid at first so the smell of the food can emit. With the dog's increased practice, you can also use fully closed lids. For some dogs, buried food cans cause them to track more intensely. Some dogs also increase their tracking speed as their track motivation becomes higher.

The different functions of food are usually inseparable in practice. When laying a training track, the handler should always consider the different functions and place the food on the training track in afore planned manner.

Tracking Terrain and Weather

Fields with and without vegetation, meadow, and any natural ground are suitable as tracking terrain. The best for the beginning handler and dog is a soft arable soil without or with little vegetation or a meadow (about 10 cm/3 inches high). Do not change the type of terrain at first. Only when your dog shows confident track behavior, can you put the training track in a different terrain. There should also be a pleasant outside temperature with a comfortable humidity and little wind. Avoid severe dryness, intense heat, strong wind or frost at the beginning.

The trial regulations state natural ground as the track terrain. This can be meadows, fields or forest soil, although forest soil is hardly ever used in trials. One should train on all possible natural terrain with as different vegetation as possible as shown to the right.

Texture of the Ground

The difficulty of a track depends, among other things, on the texture of the ground. Each terrain has its own scent and its own special difficulties. In order not to overwhelm your dog, it is important to be able to estimate the peculiarities of the different surfaces. A large part of the scent of a track in a terrain depends on the decomposition of smallest organisms and organic structures (e.g., grass). This requires water or moisture and oxygen. This means that in very dry terrain and very compacted terrain, a track is harder to smell. An extremely sandy soil is often more difficult to track (even if the track can be seen well there), especially if it is dust-dry, because there is little decomposable material (humus and microorganisms) to be found. A loamy soil is good to search in a wet state, while in a very dry state it makes high demands on the dog's tracking ability.

And not all terrain is safe for a dog. Avoid areas where insecticides, pesticides, etc. have been applied. You will know this either by smell, small grains on the ground, or fresh tractor tracks. Alarm signs are also dead plants on or at the edge of the field. Do not train on such terrain until it has rained extensively on them.

Choice of Terrain

When choosing the terrain, always keep in mind the principle: slowly increase the level of difficulty. Only when the dog masters easy terrain consistently, should you increase the difficulty.

As humans we only indirectly perceive the effect of a terrain on the difficulty of a track. The dog smells the track while we see it. And there can be a very big difference. Tracks that are clearly visible are sometimes more difficult to track, and tracks that are barely perceptible to us are more distinct in scent to the dog and, therefore, easier to track. Watch your dog as he tracks and learn what terrain is hard or easy to track for him.

Snow covered ground can also be tracked, but there is the danger that the dog learns not to track with the nose but with the eyes. A track becomes especially hard to track when there is snowfall between laying the track and tracking it.

The weather also plays an important role in training. Strong wind, severe dryness, frost and heavy rain make it difficult to find a laid track. Ideal conditions for tracking training are found in humid, not too warm weather and on a loose, not too sandy ground.

Below you will find a selection of different soils, terrains, and weather events. They are sorted by their approximate difficulty, from easy to difficult.

Terrains You Might Encounter:

- Loose arable soil (brown or light vegetation), low dense meadow
- Soft roughly plowed field
- Hard arable soil
- Terrain with very high vegetation
- Strong smelling vegetation (e.g., rapeseed)
- Very short dried up meadow
- Very hard roughly plowed field
- Hard stubby vegetation

Terrain Shape and Structures:

- Even
- Soil with tractor tracks or tillage marks
- Strongly changing vegetation (high, low, no vegetation)
- On the slope (upwind and downwind, turbulence)
- Changing wind effect (i.e., due to gusts or vegetation on the edge)

Wind Conditions:

- No wind
- Light wind
- Gusty wind
- Strong wind
- Strong gusty wind

Coarse field terrain.

Sprouted field with seed furrows.

Field with high vegetation.

Dry meadow with sparse vegetation.

A dog handler should always be aware of where the wind is coming from during training, i.e., when laying and working a track. It makes a big difference whether a dog is tracking in a headwind, tailwind, or crosswind.

> ### Determining Wind Direction
> This is how you determine the wind direction: 1) Drop a blade of grass and observe where it blows, 2) Slowly turn in a circle in one spot and notice the wind in your face.

Temperature:
- Pleasant temperatures
- Very hot
- Severe frost
- Track laid in heavy frost and thawed before tracking

Humidity
- Medium moisture in the soil and air
- Light rain
- Wet or quite dry
- Very wet or very dry
- Downpour after laying the track

Before you set your training track, assess the difficulty of the terrain and weather (especially the wind direction), and design the training track so that your dog is not overwhelmed.

Finding a suitable tracking area is not always easy. It should be a terrain where there will be no damage to the owner (usually a farmer). Of course, you need the permission of the owner to lay the track on his terrain. Talk to the owner, explaining the procedure of the training and that your dog neither will defecate nor hunt game during tracking. Take the objections of the owner seriously. In addition, it is advisable to also inform other users of the terrain. Even if they do not always have to give their consent, good cooperation and mutual information is always advantageous.

Even a relaxed waiting time has to be learned.

Calmy walking to the start of the track and picking up the scent.

Starting Routine

At the beginning of tracking training it is useful to practice an initial recurring sequence. The dog knows in the course of time that after the routine the tracking training begins. The routine helps both the handler and the dog to prepare and concentrate internally for the training. For dog handlers who also want to compete, the following routine has proven itself because it corresponds to the later situation at the beginning of a trial. Of course, you can also develop another routine for yourself.

The dog should have urinated and defecated before the training and have the opportunity to move about sufficiently. In addition, it is very useful to do warm-up exercises with the dog. Then move on to the direct preparation phase for the tracking training.

The handler puts the tracking harness on his dog if he wants to use one. He attaches the carabiner to the collar or the tracking harness and leads his dog to a helper (if possible) near the beginning of the track. The helper faces the handler. They talk to each other briefly. If the carabiner is attached directly to the collar, the handler leads the leash between the front legs and possibly the hind legs to the back and then walks with his dog to the search field or to the beginning of the track (scent pad). The dog should not drag the handler to the beginning of the track. Loud auditory signals or longer waiting times are counterproductive as they cause additional stress for the dog. The dog should learn over time to go calmly next to the handler to the beginning of the track.

Some handlers also occasionally let their dog lie down in the field for some time before a training track to simulate and practice the waiting time before some trials.

The Search Field

First, the auditory signal "Search" is conditioned. The dog is supposed to learn that he has to look for food with his nose on the ground when he hears "Search" and that he is not supposed to lift his head during tracking. Whether the dog is allowed to watch you lay the search field depends on your dog. In some dogs, watching promotes the motivation to search to a suitable degree, in others the arousal level before searching increases too strongly. These dogs are then over-motivated, and thus very quickly show an undesirable restless and unfocused track behavior.

> ### The Rectangle Tip
> Flatten a rectangle in the terrain with your shoes and place food everywhere in the rectangle. Wait at least 20 minutes, so the smell can develop. Then walk into the search area with your dog on a leash. Show your dog the food. When he has his nose down, keep praising him and repeatedly give the "search" auditory signal in a friendly manner. Stop the exercise for the dog clearly as long as there is still some food in the search field and walk your dog out of the search field. Praise him thoroughly.

Preparation of the Search Field

You can choose a field or a meadow for the search field. In the field, you can usually see the boundary of the trodden search field better. A field is also more suitable at first because the handler can see his shoe prints more easily. If you do not have arable land available, train in a meadow. The size of the food treats in a meadow should be larger than what is used in a field, so that the dog can easily find and pick them up. In addition, the area should have as few distractions for the dog as possible, i.e., no barking dogs nearby, no moving cars or similar distractions.

Create a thoroughly trodden on area, e.g., a rectangle (approx. 1.5x1.5 m or 5x5 ft for large dogs, approx.1.0x1.0 m or 3x3 ft for small dogs) and spread food that is easy to find and quick to swallow over the entire trodden area. Step into this area with a large step and after laying it, step out with a large step. No track should lead directly into or away from the search area. Memorize the boundaries of the stepped area carefully so that if necessary you can block your dog from leaving the search field by using the leash. The dog should find the food easily at this stage of training so he can focus his attention on where to find the food, not how to get the food out. However, the food should not clearly stand out from the field. The dog should learn to search with his nose, not his eyes.

Make absolutely sure that no food lies outside the search field! The dog should find the food only on the trodden area because he should learn that food is only to be found on the stepped on smelling ground and, therefore, directly on the track.

The search field was flattened beforehand.

Wait at least 20 minutes before the dog is allowed to examine the search field to allow the smell to develop.

Implement what you have learned

Lead the dog on a short leash into the search field. You also step into the search field and remain in the search field until the end of the search. If necessary, show the dog the food on the ground. The leash is loose. Give the auditory signal "Search" as soon as the dog tracks for the food with his nose close to the ground. Keep praising your dog when he shows the desired behavior. The "Search" signal is repeated when the dog tracks intensively. Additionally, praise your dog in a high, friendly voice. Hold the leash in your hand, but in such a way that it hangs loosely between you and your dog, so the dog can move freely in the search field. When praising, however, be sure to get the timing right (praise within two seconds of the desired action). Praise only when your dog is searching intensively. If the dog leaves the search field, but continues to show a focused search, do not intervene. The dog usually finds his way back to the search field by himself because only there is the treat on the ground. If the dog moves more than about 1 m/3 feet away from the search field, block the leash and point to the food in the search field. A lifting of the head will be reprimanded with a "No." Stop the exercise clearly for the dog as long as there is still food in the search field. Lead your dog out of the search field and praise him (pet him, praise him with a friendly voice, etc.).

During the search work, food can be scattered again and again. The dog should not notice this. More food in the search field means a longer search and a higher demand on the dog's ability to concentrate.

The exercise can be repeated after about 20 minutes or more at another search field. For most dogs, searching three search fields in one day is enough.

After about 10 to 20 search fields spaced out over several training sessions–distributed among several training sessions—you can tackle the next step in the training.

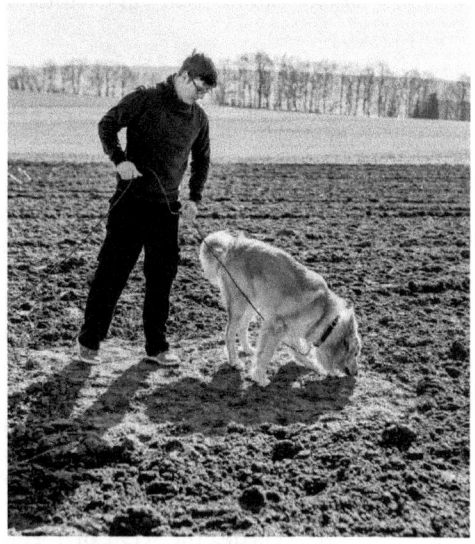

The dog searches independently on a loose leash in the search field.

Ideal Behavior of the Dog on the Search Field

The dog tracks the search field with a constantly low nose. He picks up the food without lifting his head. He swallows the food immediately and continues to search for the next piece of food with his nose close to the ground. He does not leave the search field by more than 12 inches and returns to the search field immediately by himself. Nothing (noise, movements of people or animals, smells outside the search field) distracts the dog from the search work.

Learning Goals for the Dog

- Conditioning the search signal, "Search" means to search for food on the ground with a low nose.

- The reward is only on the parts of the ground where the search field has been laid, which differs in smell from the surroundings due to the ground disturbance.

- Lifting the head is undesirable.

- Condition building: focused work over an increasingly long period of time.

- Insensitive to distraction.

- Consistent search in different terrains.

- Consistent search in different wind conditions.

- Experience of the dog: "My handler is happy when I look for the food," etc.

As with all other exercise descriptions, only a brief, incomplete list of possible undesirable behaviors follows at this point. A description of these and other undesirable behaviors, their presumed reasons, as well as the possibly necessary reactions of the dog handler can be found in Chapter 5: Troubleshooting on page 145.

Unwanted Behavior of the Dog

The dog raises his head, shows no interest in the food, leaves the search field widely with a deep nose, or he tracks for the food very frantically.

Learning Goals for the Dog Handler

The following are things that the handler should be able to perceive and observe simultaneously as he gains experience.

- Determine the appropriate food for the dog. The food must motivate the dog to search focused, it should be easy to find and quick to swallow. In addition, it should be noted that moist food attracts ants, wasps, etc., and the dog might therefore avoid the food

- Observing the effect of wind and the type of terrain on track behavior. For example, the dog also tracks in areas where there is no food because the wind carries the scent of the search field further

- Perceiving things outside the search field (e.g., barking of other dogs, people, passing cars, etc.)

- Observing the search field. Is there still enough food?

- Observing the dog: What are signs of decreased concentration (including tail position, distance of the nose from the ground, lifting of the head, etc.)

- Analyzing the dog's behavior and, if necessary, reacting to the dog's actions (e.g., blocking the leash, saying "No" when the dog lifts his head)

- Being able to assess when the dog needs support (the dog should not raise his head out of insecurity) and when he can learn to solve a problem on his own, without becoming insecure and unmotivated

- Correct timing of praise and reprimand (within two seconds)

- Repeated praise and auditory signal "Search" when the dog shows the desired behavior

- Recognition and affirmation of the dog's learning success, e.g., the dog independently returns to the search field when he has left it and picks up food there again

From Easy to Difficult

At this level, the search field can be placed in a wide variety of terrains. The differences in the smell between a meadow, rugged field or seeded field with growing seed to the untouched terrain are quite substantial. Vegetation, light humidity, weather that is not too hot, etc., support the development of smells. You will find a compilation of different types of terrain and their effect on the difficulty of a track in the chapter on tracking terrain (see p. 68). Track work is also made easier or more difficult by wind effects. The more wind there is, the more the scent of the food is blown away from the actual feeding site. Searching becomes much more difficult. Since the dog is supposed to search the search field in a focused manner and with a consistent low nose, distractions on the site increase the level of difficulty in order to search the search field correctly.

Initially, the search field should be searched without outside distractions (barking dogs, talking people, street noise, etc.) so that the handler does not need to say "No" when the dog raises his head. If your dog repeatedly tracks different search fields in a focused manner, you can place the following search fields in an area where the dog might be more distracted.

Variations to Challenge Dog and Handler

1. Only the dog is in the search field and tracks for food. The handler stands outside the search field. Here the handler only has the possibility to control the dog with his voice.

2. Unwanted behavior is not stopped or corrected. This may be advantageous for extremely insecure dogs. However, the dog does not learn what not to do.

3. It is not a rectangle that is trodden out but a ring (diameter approx. 10m/32 feet), which is also laid out with food. Here the dog moves slowly around in a circle. A second person scatters food on the track at a distance from the dog and without the dog noticing. Thus the dog builds up search stamina. The disadvantage is that the scent of the track changes constantly. The dog should not be conditioned to this.

Case Study

This example serves to deepen what has been written so far. You can lay more or less search fields at any time, also in other arrangements.

In our case study, three search fields were laid. These were searched one after the other with a certain time interval in between. The dog should be able to recover in between.

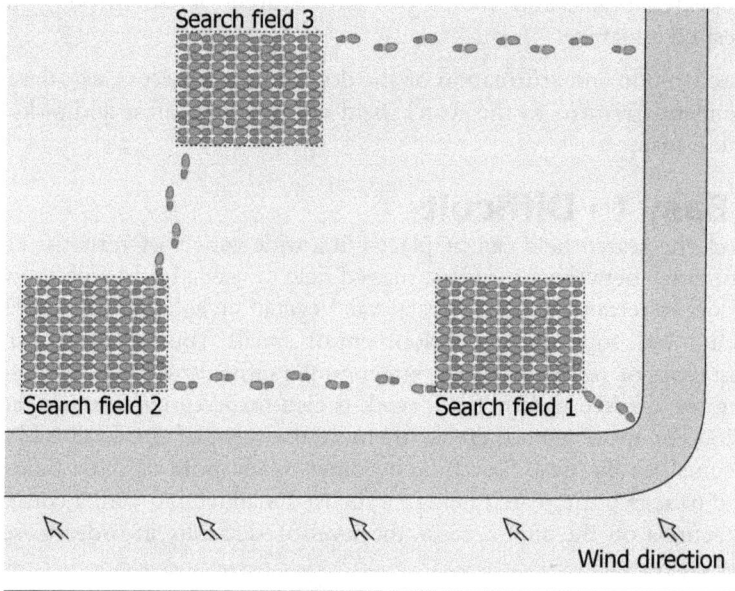

Search fields to be searched consecutively, what problems are predictable such as smelling food from another field due to the wind direction?

What foreseeable difficulties does the dog handler have to expect? Pay special attention to the wind direction!

Predictable irritations:

- The scent of food from search fields 1 and 2 is carried by the wind to search field 3, where it distracts the dog. Even if these search fields are searched first, a residual food scent remains in the terrain that can distract the dog.

- The wind blows the smell of the shoe prints into the rectangles. The shoe prints (steps) leading to the search fields are confusing because they have the same smell as the search fields, but there is no food on them. Danger of wrong conditioning. The handler must prevent the dog from following the shoe prints, even though this is exactly what he is supposed to do in the further course of the training.

- Scents along the trail (droppings and marking sites of other dogs) are carried into the search field and can be distracting.

> **For error-free learning, predictable problems should be avoided, especially at the beginning of training.**
> For example, do not place the search fields one behind another in the direction of the wind. Avoid steps leading towards and away from the search field. Approach the search field only from the downwind side.

Starting Point

The next step in the training is the actual beginning of the track, the starting field. How this is designed is described in the International Trial Regulations of the Federation Cynologique Internationale (trial regulations and current as of 2019). These trial regulations are regularly changed. In the field of tracking work, however, these changes are usually insignificant. This book is based on the trial regulations that have been valid since January 1, 2019.

For training, the handler always needs an idea of the ideal track behavior. Here is a brief description of the ideal track behavior according to the IGP:

- The dog must take the track with a deep nose and then work the track with a deep nose, high tracking intensity, consistent and steady speed.

- The dog's nose should remain close to the ground and the dog should examine every step. The track speed is even and the dog shows an intensive track manner.

- For training, this means: At the optimal track speed, the dog picks up any food immediately and shows no hasty behavior. The nose is close to the ground and the dog sniffs intensively each step. If the dog sniffs frequently to the right and left of the steps, this is an undesirable behavior and the design of the training track must be changed. Suggestions for this can be found in Chapter 4: The Training Track on page 133.

And now for the practical preparation of the beginning of the track.

Preparation

The handler imprints the starting field (scent pad). Initially, it has a triangular shape, with the scent pad marker in the direction of the following track. The marker is located to the left of the beginning of the following track. The complete starting field is trodden; treats are placed in the field. Please observe the wind direction.

The track leading away should initially only be laid with a tail wind for inexperienced dogs.

With longer tracks, the size of the starting field is reduced more and more. Eventually, the handler just stands to the right of the scent pad marker for a while, places food in the steps, and continues laying the track.

The Start Routine

The handler leads the dog to the starting point. He is next to his dog and walks with him slightly diagonally to the starting point. The dog should not get used to always going straight from the starting point. At the starting point, the handler stops next to the dog and gives the auditory signal "Search." After the start routine, the dog is prepared for the track work. The tracking line is hooked to the tracking harness (can also be done during the routine) or collar and carried under a front leg and possibly between the hind legs. The

A typical starting point.

dog should track the starting field calmly, carefully, and with his nose constantly close to the ground. He should take-in the laid out food, find the beginning of the track and follow the route of the track calmly, at a steady speed, with his nose close to the ground.

Dog at the starting point, handler waiting.   *Then the dog begins to search independently on a loose leash.*

Ideal behavior of the dog on the track

The dog should then track the starting field with a deep nose and take-in the food. If the dog has not yet learned the auditory signal "Search," the auditory signal is combined with a pointing gesture. When the dog begins to work the track, the handler first stops and then follows the dog at a distance of approx. 2-3 meters/6-10 feet. The handler lets the leash slip loosely through his hand. The distance to the dog is chosen in such a way that the dog does not feel pressure from the handler. On the other hand, the handler should also be able to effectively restrict the dog's range of motion by blocking the leash if necessary. The handler praises his dog again and again when he shows the desired behavior.

Unwanted Behavior of the Dog

The dog rushes straight ahead after the search signal without carefully tracking the starting field, the dog lifts his head, stops, does not take-in all the food, sniffs at the scent pad marker (not necessarily a mistake), or the dog shows no track behavior at all.

From Easy to Difficult

An intensively trodden starting point is the easiest to smell. This becomes smaller and less intensively trodden with increasing track experience. Eventually, it is two steps side by side without a particularly pronounced step. It is recommended, even with experienced dogs, to put food in the starting point again and again (possibly also to push the food into the ground), in order to intensify the finding of the track (see also Targeted Placement of Treats on page 87).

The starting point and the following track are easier to track if the starting point is located in a uniformly structured terrain (even field). If the terrain around the starting point is very uneven (e.g., tractor tracks), the difficulty for the dog to start tracking correctly increases. Other complicating factors that make tracking more difficult include distractions around the starting point such as high winds, game spoors, and difficult terrain.

If you want to increase the difficulty of the starting point, do not increase all difficulty factors at the same time.

For example, your dog has repeatedly tracked easy starts of the track correctly. You want to increase the difficulty. Place the next approach in more difficult terrain but not in the middle of tractor tracks, in strong wind, and greater distractions.

Things to Know

How do you estimate the difficulty of the starting point? There are no rules about what minimum distance the starting point should have to a change of terrain or path. What are the difficulties for the dog? How can you support your dog in picking up the track?

The terrain is quite dry, the shoe prints are barely visible, the ground is quite hard and the vegetation is very sparse; there are tractor tracks right next to and at the base. Each of these factors increases the difficulty in finding the starting point and the direction of the outgoing track. For further considerations we need to know the wind direction.

Let's assume the wind is blowing towards the scent pad marker. In that case, the dog can already smell the outgoing track at the starting point. That is why the starting point might not be intensely tracked.

If the wind blows in the direction of the scent pad marker, the difficulty for the dog increases because the smell of the track is blown away from the dog. If the wind blows from one of the remaining directions, the dog perceives the inconsistent terrain even more and may become more insecure.

You can make the starting point easier for your dog if you place food in the starting point and the first steps of the track when laying. Lead him to the base where the line of treats begins.

What distractions or difficult conditions will the dog encounter on the track?

Leg (Straight Line)

Preparation

The first tracks are laid with a tail wind. Otherwise, in a headwind, you might indavertenlty allow the dog to get the smell of several chunks of food at the same time in the headwind. Often he then no longer tracks in a focused manner but rushes forward. Lay the first track about 50 to 100 steps, one step behind the other. Place food in each shoe print. (See the end of this chapter for more details on placing food in a leg.) At the end of the track, place a larger amount of treats (jackpot). When not needed on the track, be advised to keep the jackpot in a lockable tin. There the food is safe from ants, beetles, and birds. Hide the jackpot, if possible.

The term "leg" is used in the trial regulations for a section of a track that is laid straight on. In the following, we use the term "straight line" instead of "leg," which describes more clearly what this section of a track is: a track that is primarily one direction. The main direction of the track is straight ahead at first, although long minor curves can be incorporated from the beginning. Wait at least 20 minutes and then let your dog work the track.

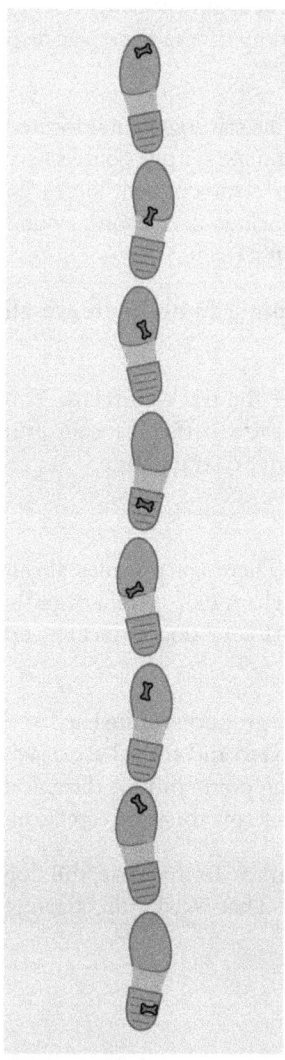

Single steps in a row with treats.

Preparation of More Straight Lines

It is our training principle to enable the dog to learn without mistakes. A tracking dog should feel successful in tracking right from the beginning of training. To achieve this, start with easy to track straight line tracks, and when the dog can track them consistently, slowly increase the difficulty. The dog should be able to master most parts of each training track without major problems. It is better to have a very easy track than a track that is repeatedly too difficult.

Major factors in the difficulty of a straight line are the type and intensity of walking, the wind direction, and the location of the treats. If you want to increase the difficulty of a straight line, do not change all the factors at once.

Track laying tips
A small starting field is laid. The scent pad marker is placed to the left of the first step. A track is laid away from the starting field. The easiest way is to lay a track in which each step is placed in front of the other, without a space between the steps. Treats are placed in each step, sometimes in the front of the step, sometimes in the back, irregularly distributed.

Steps into a field with a crosswind.

Track Laying Time

After the track has been laid, the scent of the track must first develop. Therefore, wait at least 20 minutes. Only then should your dog track the training track. Vary the lying time of the track. The IGP specifies lying times between 20 and 180 minutes depending on the trial level.

Implement what you have learned

In training, the handler follows the dog on the straight line at a distance of about two meters/six feet. The leash is slightly taut so that the handler keeps light contact with the dog. When the dog shows the desired behavior, the handler praises him again and again. Timing is important here as well. The handler observes the behavior of his dog on the straight line. In addition, he must also perceive the surrounding situation (wind direction, distractions, etc.).

Before training the dog, the handler should be aware of foreseeable undesirable behavior so he can correct them appropriately if necessary. If difficult phases of the track are foreseeable, more treats are placed on the track to make working the track easier for the dog. This always gives the dog security even when problems arise, as does praise by the handler when the dog behaves as desired.

The goal is intensive consistent track work, both on an easy and difficult track.

Once the dog is on the last straight line and reaches the jackpot, the handler clearly stops the track work for the dog. If the jackpot is in a can, the handler gives the food to the dog. He praises him with his voice, pets him, or plays with him or similar.

Finishing each track work positively is important for motivating the dog for further training tracks.

Ideal Behavior of the Dog on the Track

"The dog must take the track with a deep nose and then work the track with a deep nose, high tracking intensity, consistent and even speed. The search speed is not a faulty criterion if the dog is tracking in a convincing and intensive manner" (p. 27/28 IGP). The goal is given. The process to get there must be well thought out, so that the dog is not quickly overwhelmed and unmotivated.

Focused search on a leg, handler following 6 to 10 feet behind the dog.

Undesirable Behavior of the Dog

The dog does not follow the route of the track, he eats more than he tracks, he does not take-in all the food, he works the track very quickly, he raises his head during the track work, he often tracks with his nose outside the footsteps, he rummages more than he tracks purposefully, he tracks with a higher nose, he changes the search speed again and again, he leaves the track and moves in a circle ("circles") and much more.

Learning Goals for the Dog Handler

- To observe his dog closely: how is the posture of the tail, are breathing sounds heard, how is the posture of the head, the trunk and the muzzle? In summary: what is the dog's body language and how is it to be interpreted? What are signs of exhaustion, insecurity, distraction, stress, pain, etc.?

- To know the exact route of the track. He must know whether his dog is exactly in the track or not. Only then can he recognize undesirable behaviors on time and possibly take corrective action or change subsequent training tracks in a targeted manner.

- To perceive the direction of the wind so that he can incorporate it into his considerations.

- To perceive surrounding sounds and movements.

- To intervene on time during training (e.g., if the dog leaves the track and raises his head, say "No," block the dog with the leash, say "Search" and possibly help with a pointing gesture).

- To praise the dog again and again in time at the appropriate place, and in case of difficulties to help his dog by pointing or encouraging him in the track work.

- To correctly analyze the reasons for demonstrated undesirable behavior and make appropriate corrections.

A dog handler needs all his focus for tracking training. The multitude of all tasks can overwhelm him at the beginning. Take the help of experienced dog handlers early on and learn from their experience. After training, ask why they made certain corrections.

From Easy to Difficult

The difficulty of a straight line depends on many factors. Please do not increase the difficulty of a straight line until the dog can consistently search easier training tracks. Even then, do not increase all difficulty factors at the same time, but only increase challenges one by one. It is advised to lay the beginning of a track at the usual level of difficulty, then make the middle part of the track more difficult, and the end of the track easier again. The dog then initially finds confident track behavior, may face new challenges in the middle part of the track, but then finishes the track consistently again.

The Difficulty of a Straight Line is Determined By:

- The degree of the ground injury: e.g., does the tracker tread heavily or does he scuff his step briefly in the terrain or does he walk with normal steps without stomping, etc.

- The pace length

- The pace width

- The position of the straight line in the terrain, e.g., oblique, parallel or perpendicular to seed furrows or tractor tracks

- The soil conditions (dry, clayey, sandy, field furrow with and without vegetation, etc.)
- The wind conditions (wind direction and wind force)
- The time interval between laying and working the track and the prevailing weather conditions (drought, heavy rain, thawing ground)
- The length of the straight lines, long straight lines place a greater demand on the condition and ability to concentrate, while short straight lines give the dog little time to adjust to the conditions of the straight lines before the next corner
- Distracting factors such as wild game trails, rabbit droppings, barking dogs, cows, etc.

Difficulties due to the Degree of Ground Disturbance

The higher the degree of ground injury, the more the decomposition process starts and the more odor particles are produced. The track becomes easier for the dog to track. In very hard arable soil, you will achieve greater ground injury if you scuff while applying pressure to the shoe. If possible, you should not throw any soil crumbs to the side or to the front even when stepping harder. Even in a meadow, you will achieve the greatest ground injury if you not only stomp on but tread heavily while scuffing.

Vary the difficulty with different Designs of the Paces

The level of difficulty in working the track increases the greater the pace length and pace width.

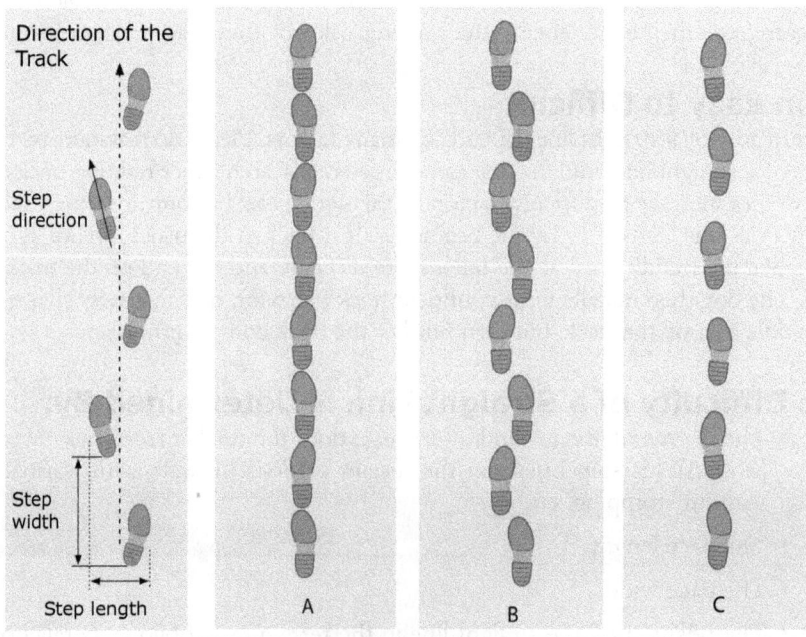

From left to right, step direction, step length, step width.

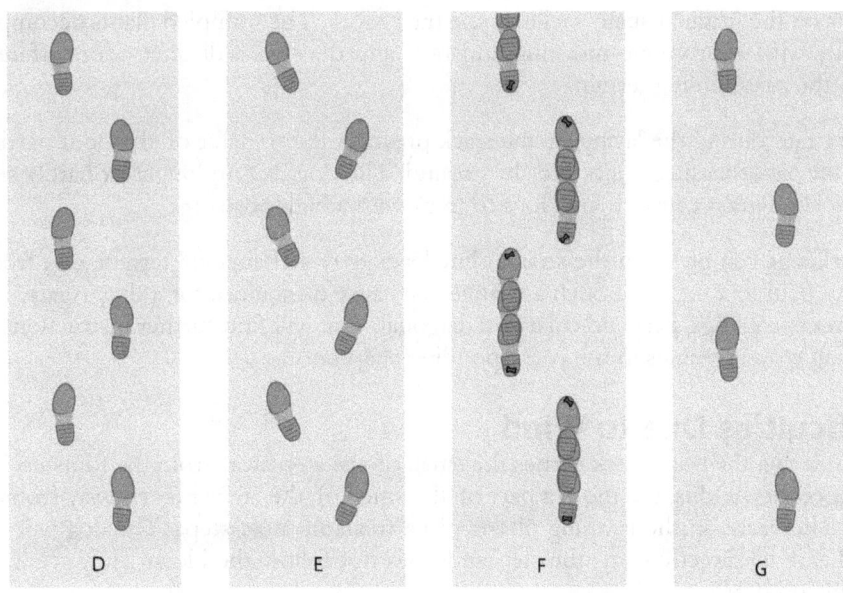

D, E, F, G represent four different step sequences.

Start first by designing the steps according to D. Then you can slowly increase either the pace length OR the pace width. Increase the difficulty only when your dog works some training tracks consistently and calmly with different wind directions, picking up all the food. He should reliably show ideal track behavior.

Step sequences E, F and G show an alternative design of the first step sequence. They are suitable for large dogs. To support the dog, put treats both at the beginning and at the end of each step, so the dog correctly learns the pendular movement right-left from the beginning of the training.

Difficulties due to the position of the straight lines in the terrain, e.g., oblique, parallel or perpendicular to seed furrows or tractor tracks.

A terrain often has visible structures that the dog can also smell. These can be tractor tracks, seed furrows, plow tracks, or the like. For most dogs, the track is harder to find if the direction of the straight line is slightly oblique to these structures. It is easier to find a straight line that is parallel or perpendicular to the terrain structures.

Difficulties due to different soil conditions and weather events (e.g., dry soil, wet soil, loamy, sandy, trampled by cultivating machines, high or low grass, rain, frost, etc.).

The odor development of a track is promoted by a not too strong soil moisture, a pleasant warmth and a not too high sand content, and is thus easier for the dog to smell. Pure sand cannot decompose and, therefore, cannot develop an odor change when walked on. Very dry and very clayey soil is also very difficult. Here the track layer can hardly cause ground injuries and thus there is hardly any change in odor development even by stepping on it strongly. Frost also inhibits odor development, especially in a terrain with hardly any vegetation.

Plants on the terrain usually facilitate the track work. The trampled plants decompose quickly with appropriate moisture and heat and develop a distinct odor difference from the surrounding terrain.

Heavy rain during the laying of the track prevents the transfer of the odor particles into the air or washes them into the ground. The dog can no longer or hardly smell them. High grass causes many dogs to track with a high nose.

A challenge can be when the straight line leads over a change of terrain, e.g., from a brown field to a meadow. Such a change can cause difficulties for a dog. Again, train different crossings, perpendicular and diagonal. You will find further instructions for training road crossings in the corresponding chapter.

Difficulties Due to Wind

Wind during the track work carries the smell of the step away from the footstep. The stronger the wind is, the more a part of the smell of the steps moves away from the step. Therefore, in the learning phase, place treats in most steps. The dog will only get this if he directly scans the step and does not follow the blown away scent (see graphic on p. 80).

Since the wind sweeps directly over the terrain, any large terrain structure (corn stalks, clods of earth, overgrowth, etc.) will cause turbulence of the wind that can cause difficulties for an inexperienced dog when tracking. Likewise, terrain formations such as slopes, drainage ditches, shrubs or groups of trees can strongly influence the wind direction. For example, if a track runs in the lee (sheltered area) of a forest and the track leads out of the lee, many dogs are initially surprised by the sudden effect of the wind and no longer follow the track exactly.

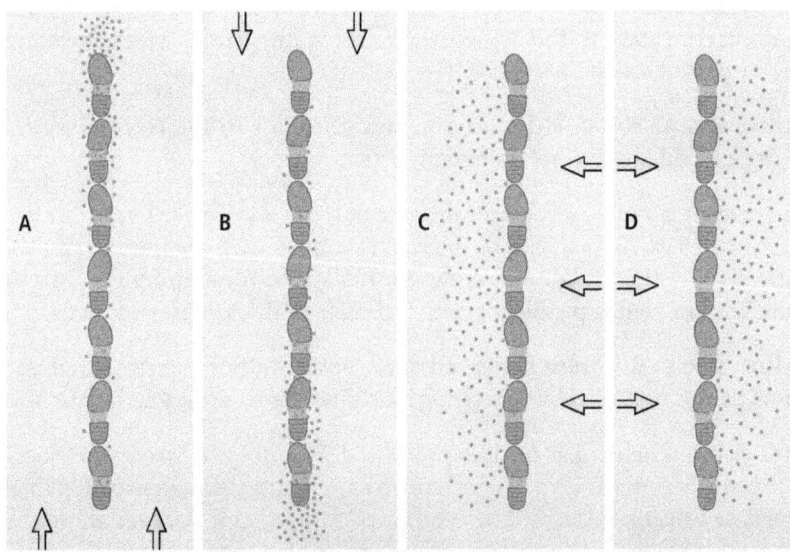

Displacement and concentration of odor particles on the track due to the influence of the wind.

When there is a headwind, many dogs lift their noses slightly, which is undesirable.

Difficulties due to a Longer Lying Time of the Track

The decomposition process is time-dependent. Initially, the rate of the decomposition process increases. In the course of time, however, it decreases. If weather conditions, such as strong heat or heavy rain, are added during the time the track is lying, a dog can hardly find the track.

Difficulties due to distracting factors such as game tracks, hare droppings, barking dogs, cows, etc.

During the track work, the dog must not be distracted from working by anything. Which distraction has a particularly strong effect on the dog depends on the character of the dog. For some dogs, barking dogs are very distracting; for a hunting dog, it is soaring birds or game tracks. You should train all possibilities. Distractions on the track such as people talking in front of or behind the dog, people in the tracking dog's field of vision (e.g., after a corner), or similar can also distract dogs from tracking.

Things to Know

In order to prevent false conditioning - dog does not directly track the route of the track but orients himself to field furrows because the track is almost always laid along a field furrow - you should vary the length and direction of the straight lines: very short (approx. 50 paces), medium length (300 paces), long (600 paces and more), different directions in relation to field furrows or terrain structures, different distance to paths, etc.

According to the trial regulations, "... a track is to be laid in a natural gait with normal steps...." and "... unnatural gait, pawing or interrupting the gait is not permitted in the entire area of the track." This is the pacing as the goal of the training, not the beginning!

Targeted Placement of the Treats

As already mentioned, the handler puts food in each step at the beginning of the training to support the optimal track manner. It motivates the dog on the one hand to track every step and at the same time gives him a positive reinforcement of his behavior.

Make sure that the food causes a high motivation in your dog. Because even if the dog eats the food on the track, it does not always lead to an increase in motivation that may be needed.

Example: A white shepherd dog storms off hastily on his first tracks, pulling strongly on the leash, and picking up only every second or third piece of food. The handler slows him down with the leash. The dog's behavior changes immediately when the type of food pieces and their size are changed.

Once the dog works the track intensively and calmly, less food can be placed in steps.

Especially with a large forward-rushing dog, which the handler can only animate to take the entire food by holding the leash, a greater distance between the pieces of food can also be useful after a relatively short time. But only if the dog still examines every step. Before that, the handler should change the size of the food, the type of treat, etc., so that the dog is eager to find each chunk of food and can pick it up more easily and with more motivation.

If you lay out less food, make sure that the food is irregularly distributed on the track. Sometimes right, sometimes left, sometimes left again, sometimes after one pace, sometimes after five paces, then three paces, sometimes at the heel, sometimes at the toe, etc.

Observe whether the treats lead to a calm intensive tracking or rather hinders this behavior. The placement of the treats should always be adapted to the behavior shown.

Directing Tracking Behavior

Food to control the track behavior is useful in, for example, crosswinds. It leads the dog back to the track again and again, so that he learns over time not to leave the track sideways. In strong crosswinds, therefore, a relatively large amount of food should initially be placed on the track during the learning phase.

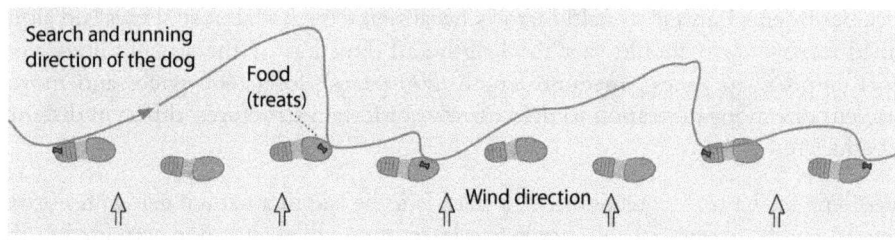

Track with food in a strong crosswind, with the line showing the predictable behavior of an inexperienced dog.

Do not reduce the food too quickly and do not stop it altogether. It motivates the dog to track and gives him confidence. Even a trained tracking dog is still motivated by food.

For an experienced intensive tracking dog, distribute the food irregularly over the track. The MAYBE of the reward, also known as intermittent reinforcement, increases his motivation. A dog that tracks only because he should or has to often does not track intensively and persistently.

> "With the help of the treats, the dog finds the track. And then he finds the treats with the help of the track." Michael Tomczak

What You Should Consider When Laying a Track

Each track layer has his way to lay tracks. If it is just one person who almost exclusively lays training tracks for the dog, he should be aware of his own patterns of laying a track and deviate from his own usual way again and again. Change the length of the pace, the width of the pace, the distance to the change of terrain or paths, and the intensity of the tread. Lay the track diagonally, parallel and perpendicular to seed furrows, change the terrain (meadow, brown field, field with vegetation, etc.). Also the length of the straight lines should be changed.

Observe the dog closely during training. The changes in the design of the training track must not lead to a general inconsistent tracking manner of the dog. Take as a rule of thumb: the majority of the beginning and end of a track should be as usual; the middle section can then be more difficult. Once in a while let another handler who is experienced in track work lay a track for your dog's training level.

Case Study

The four white lines on the above photo represent possible tracks with different expected levels of difficulty.

Straight line 3 is the easiest. It follows the direction of the seed furrows. With straight line 1, crossing the seed furrows can be confusing, but not as much as with straight line 4. Here the seed furrows run diagonally to the track direction, which is usually more difficult for the dog to track. With straight line 2, a change in the vegetation adds to this difficulty.

Terrain Change

Changes of terrain are allowed in every trial level. A change of terrain can be either on a straight line or on a semicircle of the track.

When laying the track and planning terrain change, put yourself in the dog's position at each change of terrain, tracking with the nose and not with the eyes. Depending on the wind direction, terrain edges, vegetation, etc., the dog must learn that the track leads into new terrain. Help him at the beginning by putting food in each step, showing the track or praising. The dog must adjust to the scent of the new terrain and the track when the terrain is changed. To do this, he needs a few meters or 6 to 10 feet, depending on the experience he has already had. In this area, the track should initially show no further difficulties such as a sudden change of direction.

From Easy to Difficult

For the first terrain changes, use short paces in the area of the terrain change, put food in several steps, and slowly increase the difficulty. An oblique transition to the new terrain is more difficult than a vertical transition. Train all possibilities again and again.

Case Study

What difficulties are foreseeable in the terrain changes shown in the images to the right?

Photo 1: After the terrain change, the dog may be confused by the seed lines and try to follow the seed lines.

Photo 2: Oblique transition is harder than vertical transition, dog will probably not immediately change to the terrain with high vegetation if he has never experienced this situation. He will track around the transition and only after some time follow the route of the track.

Photo 3: When tracking, the dog has a tail wind, so the terrain transition is quite difficult for the dog. The wind bounces off the edge and the dog cannot immediately perceive the further route of the track.

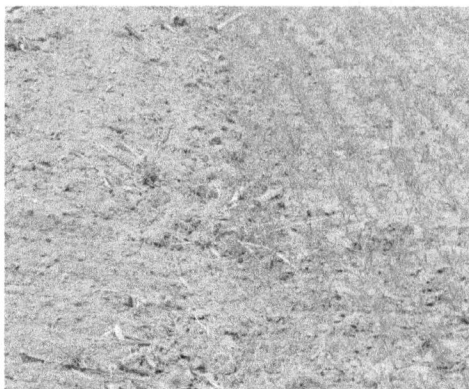

Terrain changes left to right from bare ground to lightly seeded.

Terrain changes bottom to top from bare ground to high vegetation.

Modified terrain change left to right from low ground to a field seeded with elevation. Track runs from right to left, wind blows from right to left.

Intensive tracking in front of a 90 degree corner.

Direction of the track changes.

90° Corner and Acute (<90°) Corners

A corner on the track is a distinct change of direction in the track. What does a corner mean for the dog's perception of the track? The dog, if he is attentive, perceives the changed direction of a step. He follows this direction and is thus guided to the next straight line, which may give a different scent in relation to the terrain.

> ### The more acute, the harder it gets
> As soon as the dog reliably shows the desired behavior on straight lines, even under changing environmental conditions, the first easy corners can be laid. Initially, a corner is stepped on with a large radius, which is then reduced more and more as the difficulty increases. The dog follows the individual steps when working the track, even if their direction changes.

The goal of the training is for the dog to consistently track a corner that has been laid according to the specifications of the trial regulations. These corners are laid in normal gait. The type of change of direction is also specified. Such a corner is the goal of training, not the beginning.

Dog follows the change of direction without hesitation.

Dog and handler follow the course of the track after the corner.

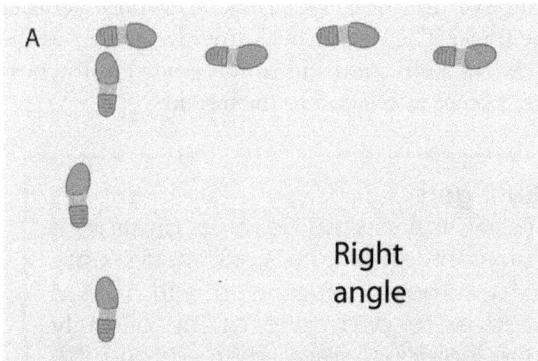

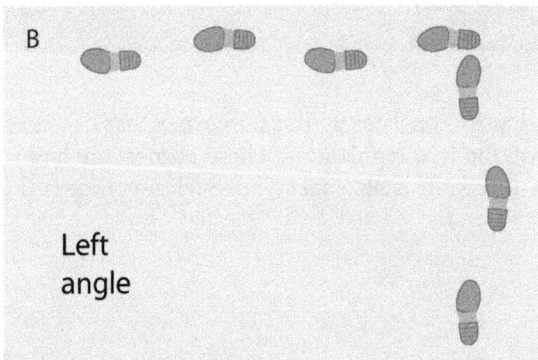

Design of 90-degree angles per IGP.

A – Angle right

B - Angle left

The training starts with very easy to track corners and only when these are tracked consistently without hesitating in all possible wind conditions, the difficulty can be increased.

Do not place food in the steps in the area of the corner because it would distract the dog's attention from the track. Food should be placed directly in the steps after the corner. An exception is a corner that is upwind. Place the food in about the third or fourth step after the corner. Otherwise the dog would notice the food too early, leave the track, and go directly to the food.

Track Preparation

Essentially, when laying corners in training for inexperienced dogs, it is important that the dog has a high probability of finding them without any problems. The handler must know exactly where the corner is and he should already plan the wind direction when laying the track. Because when working the track, a corner can be easier or harder to track due to the direction of the wind. If there is wind, then both the direction of the track changes as well as the direction of the impacting wind. Initially, lay corners with a large radius and with close pacing. Only if the dog can reliably track these corners under the influence of different wind directions and without hesitating, can you increase the difficulty of the corners, e.g., by reducing the radius, increasing the pace length or the pace width. Depending on the trial level, 90° corners respectively, also <90° corners are regulated. Initially, lay mainly 90° corners with a design very easy to track.

Implement What You Have Learned (Corresponds to Straight Lines)

In training, the handler follows the dog at a distance of approx. 2 m or 6 ½ feet. He should choose a distance so he can correct the dog if necessary. He must be able to limit the dog's radius of action. On the other hand, the dog should not feel pressed by the handler, and thus not be able to work freely and independently. The leash is somewhat taut, so that the handler keeps a good contact with the dog. At the corner he must therefore walk an arc: With a short leash a small arc, with a long leash a larger arc. The leash is slightly taut, but must not hinder the dog. Alternatively, the handler can also stop as soon as his dog turns into the next straight line and only follow his dog when the leash tightens again.

When the dog follows the track even along the corner with steady speed, the handler praises him again.

In the case of foreseeable difficult corners, food is increasingly placed on the track after the corner as a preventive measure when laying the track. This always gives the dog security even when problems arise, as does praise by the handler when the dog behaves as desired.

Ideal Behavior of the Dog on the Track

According to the IGP, the dog should consistently work out the corners. Circling at the corner is incorrect. Reassuring himself (for an explanation see the next section) without leaving the track, is permissible. After the corner, the dog must continue to track with the required high intensity and at the same speed. This description shows the desired track behavior of a dog at the corners: the goal setting. This is what we work towards in training. The IGP regulations do not describe precisely what is meant by consistently working out. The dog should track the corner at a steady speed with a deep nose and turn into the next straight line without hesitation. Consistently is usually understood as the dog standing still at the corner, while tracking the area of the corner with a deep nose also to the right and left of the actual track, but this is a clear indication that the dog has a problem with the corner. This behavior should not be shown at every corner during training because it does not meet the ideal track behavior. The corners on the training track should always be adapted to the training level of the dog and allow mostly for a track without problems. In training, the dog should take-in the food after the corner, so that he does not increase his search speed after the corner.

Learning Goals for the Dog

The dog should follow the route of the track precisely and reliably, even if the direction of the track changes and the wind comes from a different direction in relation to the track. The dog should reliably track corners of different types. He should track corners that are laid as tight or wide arcs just as accurately as 90 degree corners according to the IGP. If the dog does not immediately find the track in the area of the corner, he should stop and only track further by turning his head with a deep nose. However, small dogs often have an area that is too small for them to investigate except by turning their heads. In this case, it is usually not possible to avoid the dog moving away from the track a little in order to be able to take up the track again. However, this behavior should be an exception and should also be closely limited by the handler.

The dog should stay exactly on the track at the corner and not be distracted from it even by strong wind. The search speed must be adapted to the dog's ability to react. A dog that tracks very fast, but cannot react quickly to changes in the track such as corners or articles (no fast reaction time), will overrun any corner, even if it is appropriate for his level of training. Here the dog must learn to track more slowly.

Undesirable Behavior of the Dog

Examples of this are leaving the track in the area of the corner, shortcutting the corner, walking over the corner, losing the track, raising the head when a problem appears, circling at the corner, changing the search speed after the corner.

Learning Goals for the Dog Handler

The handler must know the exact position of the corner. Only then can he assess whether his dog has tracked the corner exactly and give him any necessary aids or signals. He must be able to read his dog's body language in order to recognize whether his dog is tracking intensively and motivated at the corner or is inattentive. The reasons for an undesirable behavior at the corner can be manifold. Therefore, the handler should be aware of several factors at the corner at the same time: the dog's body language, the wind direction, the type of corner designed by the track layer, peculiarities in the terrain at the corner (e.g., tractor tracks, changes in vegetation, etc.). The interaction of all these factors can have an effect on the track behavior of the dog and is of great importance for the consideration for further training planning. When the handler prepares his dog for a trial, he must learn how to keep the leash taut for as long as possible at a distance of 10m/33 feet in the area of a corner. For this purpose, he walks an arc at 90 degree corners, so that the leash is slightly taut, but his dog is not hindered. Some handlers stop as soon as the dog turns into the corner and only continue walking when the leash tightens again. In this case the dog must still track at a steady speed.

From Easy to Difficult

The training corners should always be designed in such a way that the dog is likely to be able to manage them well. Depending on the wind direction, some corners may have to be laid in a different pace sequence compared to other corners of the same training track, since the wind direction can pose a challenge to tracking the corner. If you want to increase the difficulty of the corners, it is best to leave the first corners at the usual difficulty level, and increase the difficulty of the corners in the middle of the track. The corners towards the end of the track are then to be laid in the easier version again. The dog can first show his confident working out of a corner, then track the more difficult corners possibly hesitantly or not quite correctly, and return to his initial confident track behavior for the last easier corners.

The difficulty of a corner depends on:
- The degree of damage to the ground by the shoe print (intensity of walking, weight of the track layer)
- The radius of the change of direction (large radius easier than a smaller radius)
- The clarity of the actual corner
- The design of the pace sequence after and in the area of the corner (see graphics A to F)
- From the direction and strength of the acting wind
- From the structure of the terrain, in flat even terrain a corner is easier to track than, for example, in a terrain with pronounced cultivation tracks, or if the corner is in a tractor track
- Wind turbulence or a change in wind direction in the area of the corner (e.g., in a roughly plowed field)
- And all factors that also influence the difficulty of a straight line (different terrain, weather, etc.)

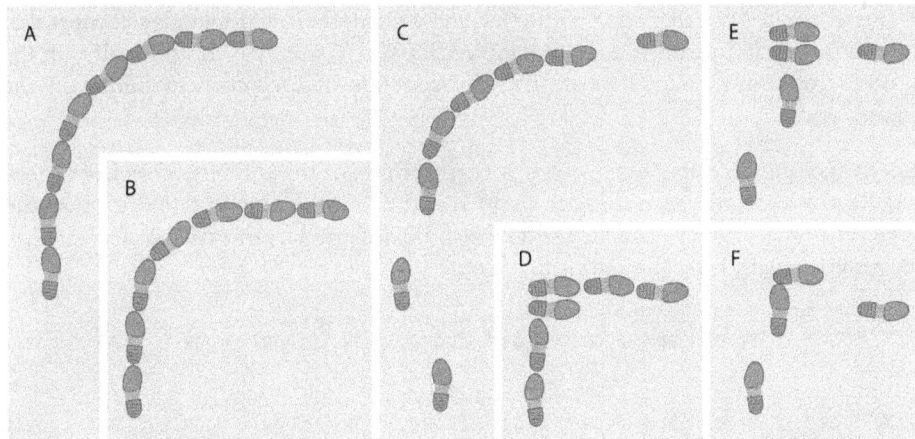

A: Corner with relatively large radius, step to step.

B: Corner with smaller radius, step to step.

C: Corner step to step, before and after the steps have a clear distance to each other.

D: Double step 90° to the running direction, important: no lateral offset, steps before and after the corner lined up without spacing.

E: Double step 90° to the running direction, important: no lateral offset, steps before and after the corner lined up with distance to each other.

F: Corner according to examination regulations.

The difficulty increases for the dog from A to F (p. 95). Of course, there are many more ways to lay a corner. The difficulty of a corner is also determined by the wind direction. Each wind direction has its own difficulties.

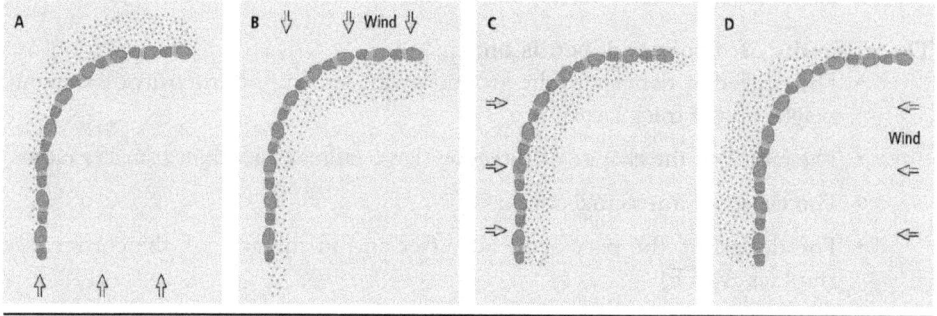

A: Dog overruns corner easily.

B: Dog turns into the corner too early, cuts off the corner.

C: Dog walks on a straight line laterally offset. If the dog does not notice in time that the scent is no longer there, he will have difficulty finding the corner because the scent will be carried away by it.

D: Dog walks on a straight line laterally offset, but the corner is very easy to find.

For optimal training, the handler should be able to assess when laying the track what problems could arise for a dog while tracking a corner. How do you lay corners that are easy to track and how can the handler SLOWLY increase the difficulty of the corners? To do this, he must know the wind direction of each corner while laying the training track.

The structure of training acute corners corresponds to the training of right corners. Initially, corners with large radii are stepped and then the radius is reduced more and more. The type of pace sequence should also be designed from easy to more difficult (see graphics A to F on the opposite page).

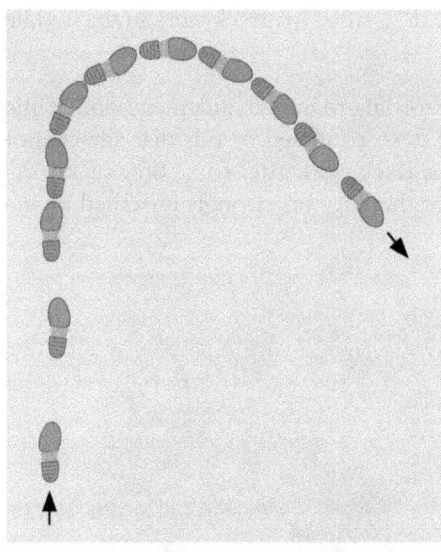

Acute corner laid with radius.

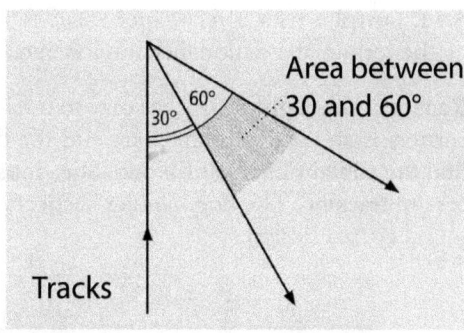

Range of an acute corner per IPG.

According to the IGP, an acute corner should be between 30 and 60 degrees.

Many dogs have to get used to tracking towards the handler when tracking an acute corner. Again, plenty of food on the track is a good way to take away the dog's initial uncertainty when tracking an acute corner.

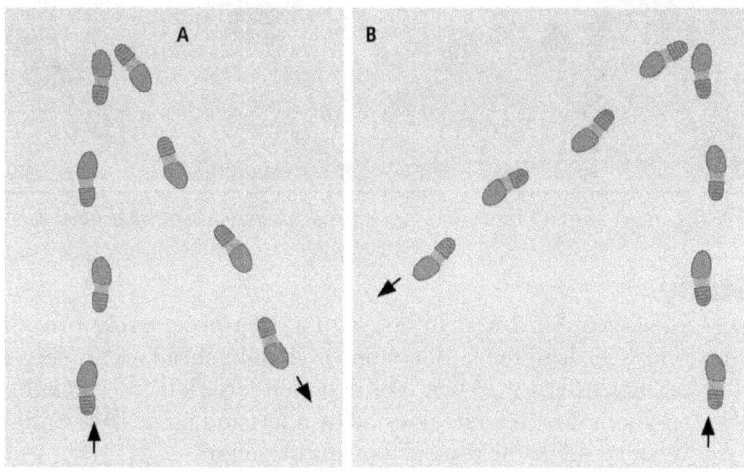

Shaping of acute corners per the IPG.

Things You Need to Know

The trial regulations do not specify the location of the corners in the terrain. They can be located near a path, a terrain edge or in the middle of the terrain. In trials, despite the specifications of the trial regulations, all conceivable forms of corners can occur, from slight bends to track breaks. Therefore, all variations should be practiced again and again. Even an experienced dog can feel unsettled by a corner that has been clearly stepped out as an arc, fail to track for the corner, and stop the track work if he is not used to such a corner design. Once in a while, let an experienced track layer lay a track for you and your dog and, thus, a different design of corners.

An Example: Sora, a very experienced female dog, stops her track work in the middle of the terrain at a national championship.

Reason: Although the track is easy to track according to human judgment, one of the corners is stepped as a small arc and the dog is so confused by this that she cannot find the straight line that follows. She stops the track work after some time of unsuccessful tracking. The dog handler suspects that the dog was strongly unsettled by the round corner design.

The dog closely observes the track at an acute angle with a somewhat lifted nose.

Case Study

A dog tracks intensively for a straight line with a deep nose, tracks over the subsequent corner (which leads to the left), continues straight ahead with a deep nose and still shows no reaction after 1 m/3 feet. The dog then turns left and comes back to the track. Only after about 2 m/6.5 feet does he turn left and come back onto the track in a large arc. What could be the reasons for this behavior?

Solution: First, we need to know the wind direction, or specify it in this example. For the following considerations, we assume that a light wind comes from the right. The undesirable behavior is composed of several different processes:

1. The dog does not notice the change of direction of the track. This can have different reasons:

    a. The dog continues to track with a deep nose, although he is no longer on the track.

    b. The dog turns left; after walking an arc, he finds the track again and continues tracking.

Solutions to 1: The dog does not notice the change of direction of the track.

This can have different reasons:

1. The dog is inattentive and therefore does not notice the corner.
2. The design of the corner does not correspond to the dog's level of training or the corner turned out to be more challenging due to weather conditions.
3. The dog has too little experience with wind.

Solutions to 2: The dog continues to track with a deep nose, although he is no longer on the track. This is probably an incorrect conditioning of the dog. For him, the desired behavior (deep nose) is not necessarily linked to tracking. This behavior is often seen in a dog whose handler does not know the exact location of the corner in training and therefore cannot correct the dog. But it can also be an avoidance behavior. The dog has the experience that as soon as he lifts his nose (for whatever reason) he expects punitive measures.

Solutions to 3: The dog turns left, and after walking an arc, he finds the track again and continues tracking. This behavior is the dog's problem-solving strategy. He was mostly over-challenged with corners in the previous training; therefore, he did not learn to consistently and smoothly track corners. He is used to tracking over a corner without reaction from the handler because the handler usually does not know the exact position of the corner. To get back on the track, the dog walks an arc and thus finds himself back on the track. As soon as the dog picks up the track again, the handler praises the dog, and is happy that the dog has picked up the track on his own. Nevertheless, it is not an ideal corner track behavior. Even the fact that the dog continues to track and find the track on his own should not hide the fact that there is a fundamental problem in the training. In further training, the corner design must be adapted to the dog's level of training and the handler must know the exact location of each corner. Tips on how a handler can remember the location of the corners can be found in the chapter The Training Track on p. 132.

The track is not visible, the starting point is near the small branch.

Deep nose doesn't always mean being on the trail.

Break In Track

In any type of corner, as well as in the design of straight lines, a break in the track must be avoided. A break in the track is characterized by the fact that if the dog follows the track closely, he has no way of noticing a change in the direction of the track. Looking at A to E, it is obvious that the first step after the corner is outside the track. Looking at B and D, the pendular (swaying) movement of the dog, especially after the break in the track, needs to be considered.

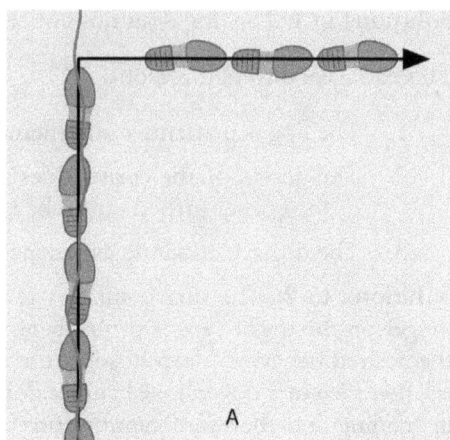

Break in track after continuous step sequence.

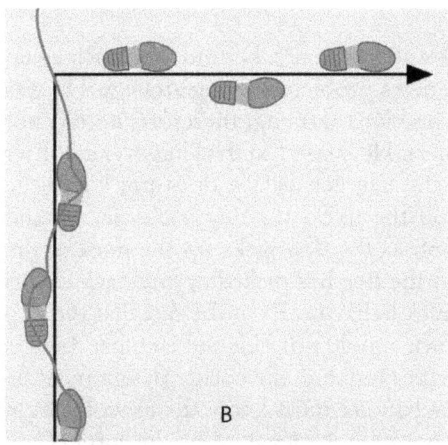

Break in track, not so pronounced.

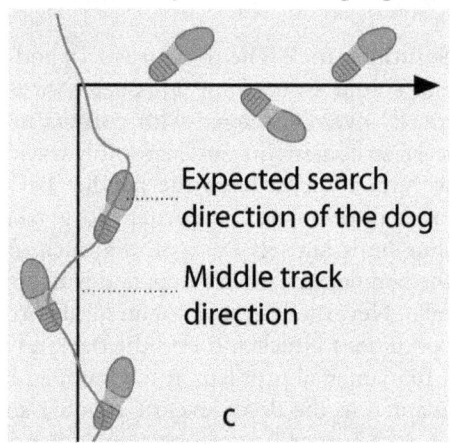

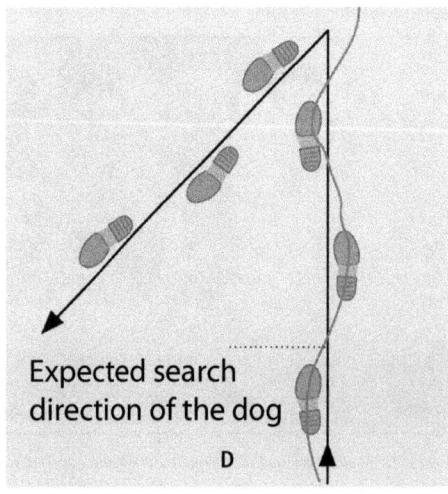

Expected search direction of the dog

Middle track direction

Break in track, pronounced.

Expected search direction of the dog

Break in track at acute corner, not so pronounced.

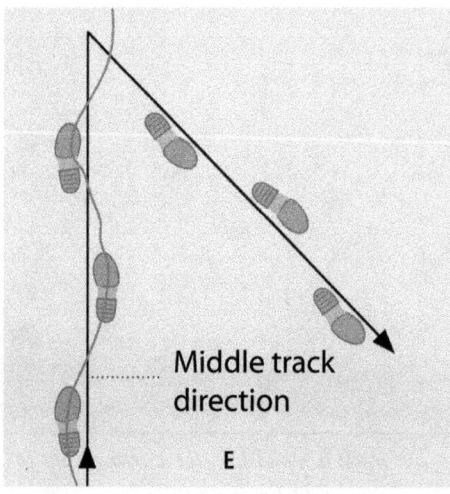

Middle track direction

Break in track at acute corner, pronounced.

Semicircles

A semicircle begins with a 90° corner and ends with a 90° corner. According to the trial regulations, it should have a radius of 30 meters. That means from the entry corner to the exit corner it is 60 meters. However, depending on the terrain and the track layer, you can find semi-circles with other dimensions and shapes. The start and exit corners of the semicircle can be as different as other 90° corners. Practice different variations.

A corner with 30 degrees is usually more difficult to track than a corner with 60 degrees. Again, occurring wind affects the difficulty of a corner while tracking. Train all possibilities again and again.

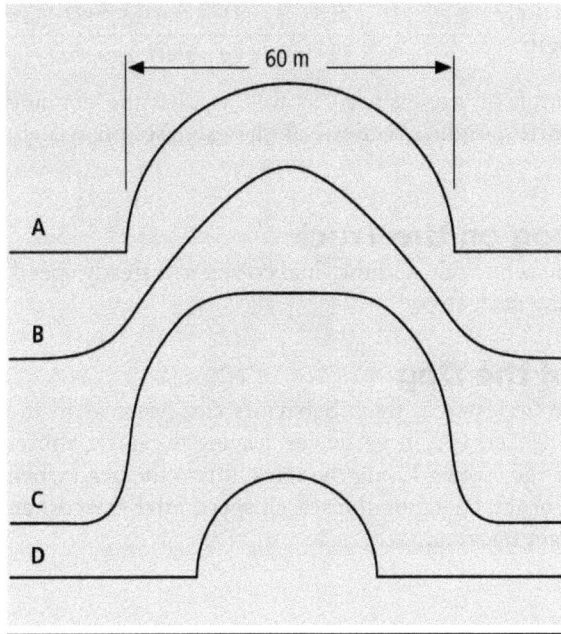

A: Semicircle with a 60-meter diameter

B: Semicircle with round input and output, angle less than 90-degrees, not a semicircle

C: Semicircle with round input and output angle and a straight middle part.

D: Semicircle with a very small radius.

Graphics A and B show acute corners according to the IGP. Strictly speaking, this type of corner design could also be regarded as a track break. In reality, such a corner can hardly be laid without spraining your knee.

A semicircle has similar challenges compared to a corner with a subsequent straight line. The only difference is that on the semicircle, in contrast to the straight line, the wind direction constantly changes in relation to the track direction. In addition, the track constantly changes in relation to the prevailing orientation of the terrain (e.g., seed furrows or mowing tracks). Therefore, it is to be expected that the dog will always deviate slightly from the track. In order to be able to correct the dog, an exact knowledge of the track course is also important here.

Track Preparation

In the area of the semicircle, you need to put a lot of food in the steps during the learning phase, so the dog can gain confidence and help him find the track again in case he deviates from it. Many dogs feel unsure due to changing wind impact and constant change of track direction in relation to the terrain. Even when a dog consistently tracks a straight line with relatively big pace length, it is recommended to at first lay a semicircle with an easier, i.e. smaller, pace length.

Searching on a short sown field.

For further preparation and execution of the exercise, as well as what the dog and handler should learn, review the corresponding sections of the exercises on straight lines and corners.

Ideal Behavior of the Dog on the Track

The dog tracks the entry corner, the semicircle and the final corner at a steady speed, with a deep nose, intensively tracking each step.

Undesirable Behavior of the Dog

When tracking a semicircle, all the undesirable track behaviors can occur as in the sections on tracking a straight line or a corner, in particular: leaving the track, abbreviating the semicircle, tracking over the corner, losing the track, lifting the head when a problem appears, circling at the corner, changing the search speed after the corner, rummaging behavior instead of exact tracking.

From Easy to Difficult

The difficulty of a semicircle is increased by, among other things:

- Strong and/or gusty wind
- Clear terrain structures (tractor tracks, machining tracks, etc.)
- Large pace length
- Large pace width
- Smaller radius of the semi-circle
- Lower intensity of soil injury
- For more descriptions of difficulty factors, see the sections on straight line and corner work

Case Study

What difficulties should you expect at points 1 to 10?

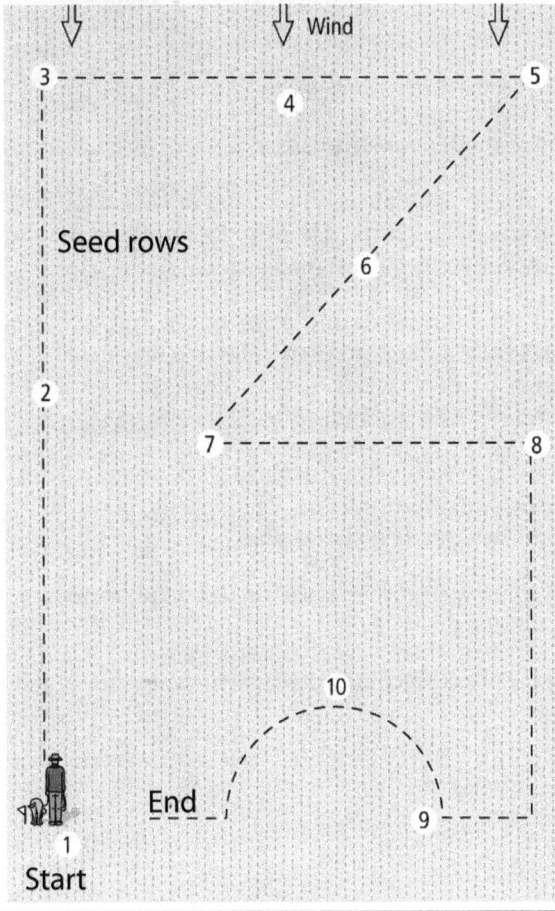

What are the foreseeable difficulties?

Before you can start solving this problem, you need to know the prevailing wind direction. At the first straight line, the wind comes from the front. The following is a selection of the possible difficulties. These may or may not occur.

Point 1: The track begins in the headwind; the dog immediately smells where the track leads but does not intensively take the starting point; instead he immediately rushes forward.

Point 2: The track begins in the headwind; the dog lifts his nose slightly upwards and smells the laid out food and becomes a little faster when tracking. The direction of the track is easy to track along the terrain (seed line).

Point 3: Because the corner is perceived early, the dog turns too early and abbreviates the corner.

Point 4: When the wind comes from the side, the dog mistakenly works the track as it has seemingly shifted laterally to the right. The direction of the track is at a 90 degree corner in relation to the terrain structure which makes it easy to track.

Point 5: When the wind blows the scent of the track away from the dog, the corner is relatively hard to track. The dog may circle. If the direction of the track is oblique to the terrain structure, it is more difficult to track.

Point 6: When the straight line is oblique to seed lines, the dog has difficulty following the route of the track. He may try to follow the direction of the seed lines, walks shifted to the left (crosswind).

Point 7: When the wind blows the scent of the track away from the dog, the corner is relatively difficult to track. The dog may circle at the corner but the new direction of the track is now 90 degrees in relation to the terrain structure and thus is easier to find.

Point 8: The corner is relatively difficult to track because the wind blows the scent of the track away from the dog. The new direction of the straight line along the terrain structure is easier to find.

Point 9: This is an easy corner because the wind blows the scent of the straight track towards the corner.

Point 10: Because the semicircle is in structured terrain, the dog may try to follow the direction of the seed lines.

An intensive search with a strong pull on the leash

1. Dog intensively searching the track.

2. The dog indicates by lying down.

3. The dog handler stands next to the dog.

4. "Search," the dog continues to track extensively.

Indicating Articles

In addition to working the track, the dog's task is also to indicate articles that the track layer has previously placed on the track. The dog should make it clear to the handler that he has found an article. He does this by indicating with body movements or by picking up the article in his mouth. Picking up is very unusual. The preferred indicating is that the dog either stops in front of the article standing, lies down, or sits down. The most common way to indicate is lying down as shown above. The dog is supposed to calmly remain in the chosen position until the handler takes the article and gives the auditory signal "search." The size of the articles is specified in the IGP (length 10 cm/4 inches, width 2-3 cm/.75-1.8 inches, thickness 0.5 to 1 cm./.2 to .4

inches). They should consist of different materials. The articles must not be clearly different from the terrain (in the trial practice they sometimes are). When indicating an article, it should be between or directly in front of the dog's front paws.

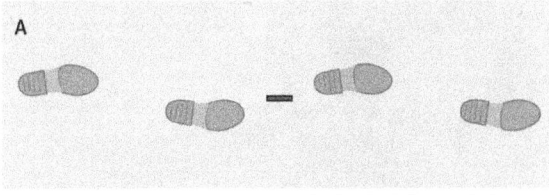

The article lies between the steps in the direction of the track.

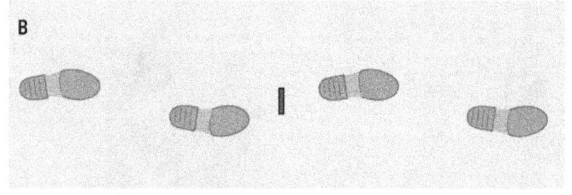

The article lies between the steps, perpendicular to the track.

The Beagle indicates by standing still.

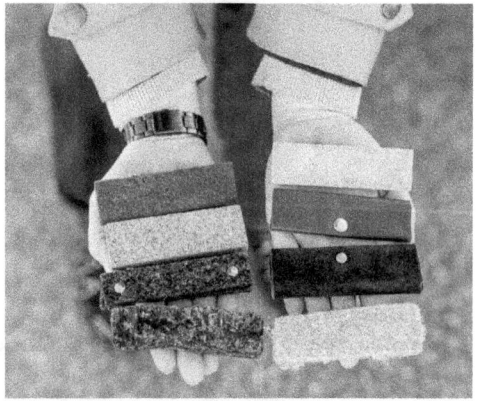

A variety of articles.

The Malinois indicates by sitting.

> **Make contact with the articles prior to laying the track.**
> On a track, articles are laid out by the track layer. The dog must find them and either pick up or indicate. New and already used articles may be used, but they must be worn on the body by the track layer at least 30 minutes before laying down. The items are placed between the shoe prints according to the IGP.

Preliminary Considerations and Exercises

The handler must decide how his dog should indicate the article, preferably by standing, sitting or lying down. Each method has its advantages and disadvantages.

Indication Type	Advantage	Disadvantage
Lying down	Dog remains securely in the position, the inhibition to continue tracking without the handler's auditory signal is higher than in the other indicating positions.	For many dogs, it is very unpleasant to lie down on wet ground, also unpleasant on hard ground vegetation. High susceptibility to undesirable behavior: slow lying down, oblique indicating.
Sitting	This is a relatively stable indicating position. Dogs that pull their hind legs towards the front legs when sitting down can take a correct position towards the articles.	Wet ground and hard ground vegetation are unpleasant, but not as much as when lying down. Possible problem: some dogs pull thier front legs backward when sitting down, thus the distance to the articles is too big.
Standing	This position avoids reaction of dog to wet or uncomfortable terrain.	For some dogs, a very unstable position. Dog continues to track more easily, possibly without auditory signal, than with other indicating positions. High susceptibility to faulty behavior with regard to calm and stable standing. Dog often sits or lies down when handler steps next to him.

Appropriate Time to Start "Indicating" Training

The dog should show a consistent track of straight lines and corners in different types of terrain and weather conditions. Then the "indicating" training on the track can be started. If you start the indicating training too late, some dogs show a very unwilling indicating behavior, which is very difficult to improve. The dogs then prefer to track the track rather than find articles. Outside of the track, indicating can be practiced earlier.

Preparing the Track

The track layer places the articles on the track. He must know exactly where the articles are located, even later when working the track from a distance of 2-10 m/6-32 feet behind the dog.

At the beginning of the indicating training, the article should be very easy for the dog to find. Place the article directly in a shoe print because the dog will thoroughly track the shoe print (during the normal track anyway) and will automatically perceive the article. Later the articles are placed between the shoe prints, sometimes lengthwise, sometimes crosswise to the track direction. According to the IGP, the articles must be placed between the shoe prints. However, it is to be expected that the articles will be partly in or sometimes next to the prints. Therefore, gradually train all conceivable possibilities.

Implement What You Have Learned

Indicating is made up of many different behaviors, each of which is very error-prone. You will find descriptions of the different ways to teach the dog to indicate an article below. From the beginning, make sure your dog behaves correctly at the article. Refer to Chapter 5: Troubleshooting, page 182 for ways to address problems that arise.

Learning Without Outside Help

The dog already knows and obeys the auditory signal "sit, down, or stay" outside the training track. As soon as the dog's nose is on the article, the handler blocks the dog with the leash and calls an auditory signal such as "down." If the dog obeys the auditory signal, he is praised. The handler must be sure that his dog has perceived the article. Only then will the dog associate the article with the auditory signal and the desired behavior.

Learning with Pre-exercise Outside the Track

The dog first learns to indicate articles correctly off the track.

For example, the dog is to indicate an article by lying down. To do this, you lay out the articles visibly; signal to the dog through a pointing gesture that he should lie down in front of the article. You can also hold food in your hand to support the pointing gesture. When he is about to lie down, give an auditory signal. As soon as he has taken this position, praise him and/or give him food immediately. Make sure the article is between his paws. Repeat this procedure at each article until the dog begins to lie down at the article by himself. You can also use the "Down" auditory signal at the beginning of the exercise if the dog has already mastered it. However, if the dog has been forcefully taught the "Down" auditory signal, do not use this auditory signal with sensitive dogs during tracking training. It puts the dog under unnecessary pressure.

When the dog is reliable in indicating articles outside the track, the first articles can be put on the track. Here, too, help your dog with pointing gestures combined with food in the hand and auditory signals if he does not indicate despite the preliminary exercises. There are few dogs that can spontaneously transfer indicating outside the track to the situation on the track.

Learning with Clicker Training

The use of a clicker is particularly suitable for indicating training. The handler and the dog should already have experience in clicker training. With clicker training, the dog receives a precise signal that shows him that he is behaving correctly. The clicker signal has been previously conditioned with something pleasant (usually food) and signals to the dog that the behavior shown is desired. The clicker signal is motivation for the dog to continue to perform the behavior shown because it promises a reward. If you do not already have experience with clicker training but would like to apply it, you can read about it in specialized literature on clicker training and practice it in everyday life.

Learning with Outside Help

A helper leads the dog on the leash during tracking. The handler walks next to or behind the dog. Shortly before the dog's nose reaches the article, the handler steps next to his dog and bends down to the article. With food in his hand, he points to the article and makes the dog take the desired position. At the same time he gives an auditory signal, e.g., "down." As soon as the dog has taken the desired position, he gives the dog the food and praises him. The article should lie directly in front of or between the paws.

The handler holds food at the location of the article.

Helper holds the leash, handler is next to the dog.

One advantage of the clicker is that when indicating, the handler is in front of the dog with his hand, so that the dog does not turn around to him. The desired behavior is shown to the dog by the handler. The dog's movement sequence during indicating must always be the same. This is ensured by the handler's help. Only after many repetitions are the aids (auditory signals and pointing gestures) reduced. For example, the handler no longer points to the article but may still give an auditory signal. If the dog continues to indicate quickly without hesitation, the auditory signal can also be dismantled. Support your dog at the slightest hesitation with a clear auditory signal or pointing gestures.

Behavior of the Handler After Indicating

In the following, indicating by lying down is described. The behavior of the dog handler when indicating sitting or standing is analogous to those positions. We have the situation that the dog has just indicated the article and the handler is right next to him. The handler praises his dog as soon as he lies down and gives him food.

If the dog is already indicating an article when the handler is a few meters/10 feet behind him, the handler drops the leash and walks either to the right or to the left of his dog. He should not always walk to the front of his dog on the same side. Unfortunately, the danger is that many dogs then turn to the side where they expect the handler to come when they are indicating. As soon as the handler reaches the dog, he gives him food on the article as a reward. He must already have this food in his hand while walking forward. If he only takes it out of the pocket next to the dog, the dog may become restless and there is a risk that he will change his position.

The handler takes the article in his hand, slowly gets up, and holds this article upwards. When getting up, the handler must make sure that the dog remains still. He supports this with pointing gestures and a friendly "Down" or "Stay."

After that, he puts the article in his pocket. Then he can pet the dog as a reward or give him some food. While doing so and without being noticed by the dog, the handler puts food in the next step. If the dog notices the food, he must not pick it

The right hand of the dog handler stays in front of the dog.

The handler places treats by the article as a reward.

up. The handler takes the leash in his hand (it must remain loose), stands next to his dog and waits 3 to 4 seconds. He points to the track (only during the learning process) and gives the auditory signal "Search." If the dog does not get up, he can pull lightly on the leash or show the dog the track again with his hand. The dog then continues the track with a deep nose. He is motivated to do this by the food that lies in the next shoe print. The handler stays standing at first and follows his dog after approximately 6.5 feet with a loose or slightly taut leash. The handler can also pet the dog first, give him food, and then take the article. Observe your dog to see which order allows or encourages him to remain calm.

As the dog's confidence in indicating progresses, the distance between the dog and the handler should be increased right before the article is indicated. The dog must get used to the fact that it takes some time for the handler to reach him. This waiting time must not unsettle him.

Ideal Behavior of the Dog on the Track

- According to the IGP, the articles must be "convincingly" indicated. The term "convincingly" can be interpreted in different ways. Mostly it is understood as an immediate and fast indicating (laying down, sitting down or standing) when reaching the article. For some time now, it can be observed during trials that the dog rigidly fixates on the article when indicating. This dog's behavior is practiced in training. However, it puts the dog under a permanent tension. This is not desirable.

- Indicating must be done straight in the direction of the track. Slightly oblique indicating is not faulty (note: what is oblique depends on the interpretation of the judge).

- The article must be directly in front of or between the front paws.

- The dog must remain calmly in the indicating position until he receives an auditory signal to continue tracking.

The dog should not only find the article but the regulations state exactly how the dog should act after finding the article. During trial, the handler is not allowed to give any help to his dog while indicating. Petting is allowed. When training indicating, it is

Article is between the front paws of the dog, correct.

The article is in front of the dog, incorrect.

important from the very beginning to have a correct procedure of indicating. Incorrect behavior is very difficult to change. That's why you should think carefully about what correct indicating looks like and how you want to teach it to your dog.

Undesirable Behavior of the Dog

Article is not indicated:

Item next to dog, incorrect.

- Dog indicates although there is no article on the track.

- Dog indicates the article too early, i.e., the article is clearly too far in front of the front paws.

- Dog indicates the article obliquely to the track direction.

- Dog indicates slowly, e.g., lies down slowly or delayed or first with the chest and then with the back.

- Dog walks around the article and continues to track.

- Dog hesitates briefly at the article but continues to track over it.

Learning Goals for the Dog Handler

The handler should know exactly the location of the article. Only then is correct timing possible for him and he can react correctly and on time. For example, if there is no article on the track, but the dog nevertheless indicates an article, the handler should ask his dog to continue tracking. He should not step to the dog's side and only then notice that there is no article between the dog's paws.

The handler should keep an eye on the wind direction. The scent of articles is perceived by some dogs over relatively large distances in headwind and they then tend to indicate too early. Here it is important to react appropriately and not to assume indicating without an article.

The handler must notice when his dog shows insecurities when indicating. He should help him and not assume that the dog will indicate the next article correctly. With the next articles, he must closely observe his dog. Does he hesitate before reaching the article, does he even start to avoid it? Does his dog's behavior depend on the material or the location of the article? For more details on appropriate corrective actions, please refer to Chapter 5.

Auditory signals must be given on time. At the moment the dog perceives the article, the auditory signal for the desired indicating position should be given ("Down," "Sit," "Stand"). If the auditory signal is repeatedly given too early or too late, the dog will probably not reliably learn the desired quick indicating behavior. It is a challenge for many dog handlers to give their dog the right help at the right time during indicating training. Use the experience of a competent trainer here as well. A handler may need a lot of patience to teach his dog the correct indicating behavior.

In case of doubt, do not assume that your dog does not want to indicate, but that he has not understood what to do. Give him the necessary help and do not let him stand at the article in uncertainty.

From Easy to Difficult

- For most dogs, an article located in the shoe print is easier to find than an article located between prints, especially in terrain with taller vegetation.

- Articles lying lengthwise to the track direction are usually more difficult for the dog to perceive than those lying crosswise.

- Dogs react differently to different materials. Some dogs indicate everything without any problems, others have difficulty recognizing and indicating certain materials. Green articles in green overgrown terrain are often not perceived as articles by many dogs at first.

- Articles that smell like different people are not actually more difficult than the ones the handler always uses. They are just unfamiliar. If you use only articles that smell like you for an extended period of time, you may be encouraging incorrect conditioning in your dog. Frequently also use new articles during training. Give them to another person for about 30 minutes or longer and then store those in a plastic bag until being put on the track.

- A dog may not indicate articles that are in the field but not laid out by the tracker. Train this as well. Use things that are already lying in the terrain and lay the training track over them.

- It is particularly difficult for some dogs to correctly indicate articles in a head-wind. Many dogs indicate as soon as they smell the article. They, therefore, usually indicate articles too early in a headwind, unless the dog has already understood that the article must be between the front paws or just in front of them.

- If a dog has difficulty in tracking the track, he is more inclined to overshoot an article.

More Things to Know

In trials, it sometimes occurs that a track layer tramples down a small area of tall grass where the article will be placed and then places the article there. He means well because the dog can find the article more easily. However, many dogs are confused by this way of laying and don't really know if this is an article they should indicate or not. It doesn't fit into their previous experience of what the environment of an article on a normal track should look like. Therefore, train this version as well.

Indication Training Summary

Indicating training is complex and error-prone in its process. Therefore, here is a list of ideas. You should:

- Start indicating training as soon as the dog shows consistent track behavior
- Always demonstrate a lot of patience
- Use high value treats at the article as a reward
- Plan small learning steps when learning the movement sequence
- Consider when the indicating behavior is not quite correct, between "main point: indicating" (no correction) and "correct indicating" (with corrective action)
- Use lots of praise while making sure the dog remains calm
- Continue giving aids for a long time: possibly pointing to the article as soon as the dog has reached it, blocking the leash when the dog has reached the article (possibly by a helper)
- Train the auditory signal "Point" (dog touches article with nose) outside the track; it can be used if the dog indicates too far away from the article
- Train different articles
- Train different positions of the article in relation to the track
- Advance sometimes to the right and sometimes to the left of the dog
- Note if the article is not between the paws or directly in front of them, do not put the article in the correct position to the dog afterwards
- Consistently forbid the dog to touch the article (Attention: Avoid avoidance behavior at all costs)
- Adapt the type of indicating to the type of dog
- Consider clicker training which can be very helpful

The handler holds the article up high.

The dog continues to track intensively.

The dog momentarily checks out a cross track.

After a short detour the dog continues to track confidently.

Cross Tracks

A cross track is a laid track that was laid after the training track and crosses it several times. The dog must not follow this cross track. A cross track is only laid in the IFH-1, IFH-2 and IGP-FH trial levels. Cross track training should only be started when the dog shows confident track behavior, consistently works out corners, and quickly and consistently indicates articles. Often cross track training initially unsettles the dog.

When Tracks Cross

The training track (original track) is laid. After at least 30 minutes, another track (cross track) is laid that crosses the previously laid training track. Both tracks can be laid by the same person during training. After another minimum of 30 minutes, the dog works the training track. The dog should follow the training track at the intersection of the training track and the cross track.

The time interval between the cross track and the original track is specified in the trial regulations. The cross track should always be laid half an hour before the trial track is tracked. In training, different times (longer or shorter) should be trained. Most dogs can smell this difference. The minimum distances between the cross track and the corners of the original track are specified in the trial regulations. Again, reality is often different. Train all possible variations.

A trial cross track must have a distance to the corner of 40 paces. It must not lie on the first or second straight line. It must not intersect the straight line at an angle of less than 60°. And when the cross track layer goes to the cross track intersection, he must have a distance of at least 10 m/32 feet from the original track. Here, too, the following applies: Train all possibilities, including angles less than 60 degrees.

The dog begins to work on the cross track.

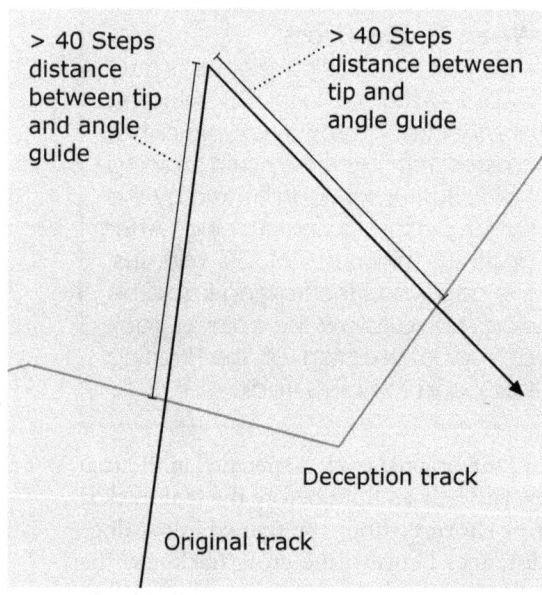

> 40 Steps distance between tip and angle guide

> 40 Steps distance between tip and angle guide

Deception track

Original track

Specification of IGP of where and how the cross track should be located.

How Can the Dog Distinguish Between Tracks?

The cross track and the original track are laid at different times. The scent of the track develops and changes in the course of time, so that the original track differs in smell from the cross track. In addition, the track is laid by a different person than the original track during a trial.

For our training, we want to condition the dog mainly on the different smell of the laid tracks. Therefore, the same person can lay the cross track as the original track during training. If there is a difference in the individual scent added, most dogs will not have any problems. To be on the safe side, have another person lay a cross track for you from time to time. Observe your dog closely to see if he then shows a change in behavior.

Cross Track Opinions Differ

It is controversial among dog sportsmen whether or not the dog should practice ignoring a cross track right away. Many are of the opinion, "The dog should just stay on the track." However, experience shows time and again that without specific cross track training, a dog is more likely to switch from the original track to the cross track. On the other hand, a dog may track with his nose even slightly off the track more often as a result of cross track training. He becomes more sensitive and, therefore, sometimes a little more restless in his track behavior. This is not desired in dogs that train tracking as part of the utility dog trial. In these trial levels, no cross tracks are laid and, therefore, usually not trained.

Some dog handlers think that if their dog does not notice the cross track or indicate it, this is a sign that they do not need to train ignoring cross tracks. Most of the time this is a false conclusion. Depending on the wind direction and the intensity of the cross track, your dog may sometimes switch from the original track to the cross track.

At track trials on a regional level (e.g., in dog sport clubs), the cross tracks are often laid in such a way that the dog will probably not notice them. At supra-regional trials, the majority of the cross tracks are true cross tracks, which are sometimes more obvious for the dog to smell than the original track. The danger that the dog will switch to this cross track is very high without successful cross track training.

Preparing The Tracks

The original track is laid. In the area of the planned cross tracks, it should be easy to track, so that the dog can consistently track the original track. The track layer puts a stick next to the track at the planned cross track point so that the track layer (or another person) knows later exactly where the original track is. Only then can the cross track intersection be designed in a targeted manner. After an appropriate period of time, the cross track is laid so that it crosses the original track several times.

Initially, no food is placed on the planned crossing point when the original track is laid. Only when the cross track layer lays the cross track over the original track does he throw food into the steps of the original track after the crossing. As soon as the dog continues to track the correct track after the cross track crossing, he is rewarded by the food that has been laid out and regains confidence in tracking the rest of the track.

If there is a headwind, the dog may smell the food before the cross track crossing, be somewhat distracted by it, and prefer to continue tracking straight ahead. In the best case, the dog will still perceive the cross track.

Implement What You Have Learned

When laying the cross track, the stick is used again. The handler follows his dog at a training distance. He must know exactly where the cross track crosses the original track.

Ideal Dog Behavior of the Dog on the Track

The dog is allowed to indicate and test cross tracks if he does not leave the track.

In practice, the dog may stop, check the cross track briefly to the right and left with a deep nose without leaving the original track, and then continue tracking intensively with a deep nose.

Learning Goals for the Dog

The dog learns to distinguish the scent of the original track from the scent of the cross track and to follow the course of the original track. If he tests the cross track with his nose, he should stand and not leave the track.

Undesirable Behavior of the Dog

The dog changes from the original track to the cross track, he raises his head, he circles at the cross track intersection.

Learning Goals for the Dog Handler

The handler learns to recognize the problems his dog has in the learning process of distinguishing between the original track and the cross track. He must be able to judge when his dog needs help to show the desired behavior and when the dog is likely to be able to solve the problem on his own.

He must never leave his dog standing on the track with his head up, hoping that he will eventually exhibit the desired behavior. An insecure dog is quickly demotivated.

If the dog wants to continue tracking on the cross track, the handler blocks the leash and thus limits the dog's range of movement. If necessary, he can support this with a "No," and show the dog the original track.

Cross track training presents the dog with a problem to solve. Each dog has a different behavior to solve problems. Some become frantic, others stop in uncertainty and seek the handler's help. Watch your dog to see what behavior he exhibits. He should remain calmly on the track, possibly briefly (one pace wide) follow the cross track with his nose, and then return to the original track. Support your dog in this behavior.

From Easy to Difficult

The following influences, among others, will determine the difficulty of a cross track:

- The position of the steps of the original track and the cross track in relation to each other. If the steps of the cross track are in the narrower area of the original track, the other direction of these steps will lead the dog to assume a corner of the original track.

- The difference in the degree of decomposition of the original track and the cross track (strong or weak or scuff steps, different time duration of the decomposition process).

- The direction of the wind when tracking the track and the direction of the wind in relation to the cross track.

- The corner at which the cross track intersects the original track.

Positioning of the Steps and Direction

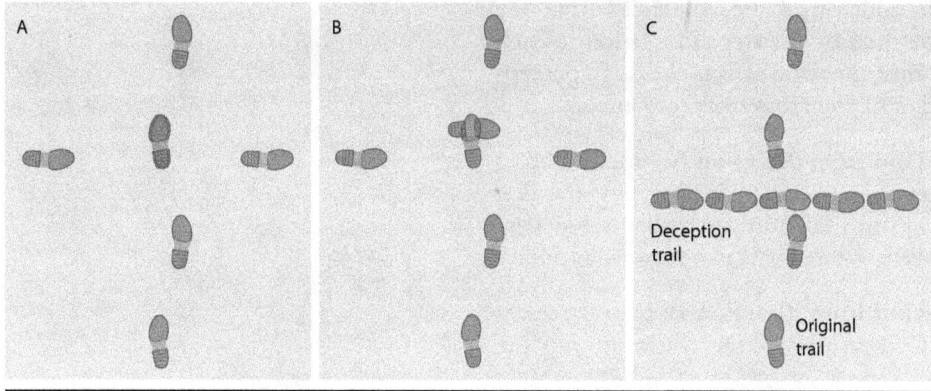

A: Footprint found on the cross track. This is seldom encountered.
B: Footprint on the cross track. This is seldom encountered.
C: Several footprints on the cross track. This is encountered more often.

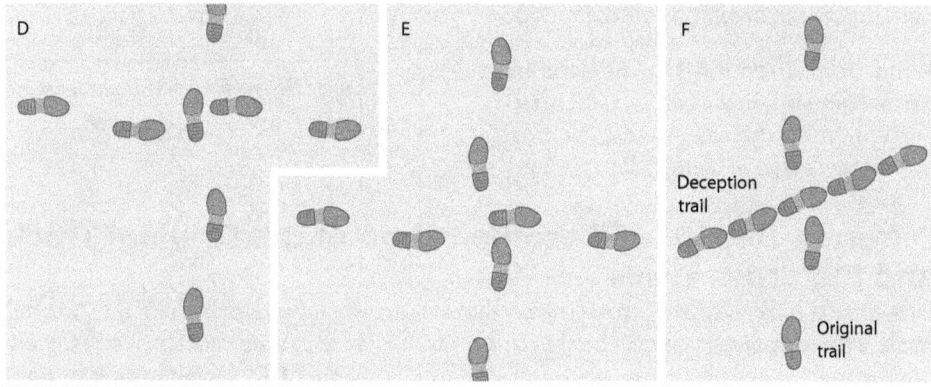

D and E: Footprints of the track and cross track form a corner making it hard to follow.
F: Several footprints of the cross track found in the area of the track, oblique to the track.

Influence of the Wind

In addition to the influences from the position of the steps in relation to each other, the wind affects the dog's perception of the cross track (see image).

Wind from direction A: Smell of cross track comes from behind left, the dog will turn left (however, this is not very likely as the dog is in a forward motion).

Wind from direction B: Dog perceives the cross track in the headwind early on.

Wind from direction C: Dog will turn to the right because the dog perceives more strongly the scent of the cross track approaching the track from the right due to the favorable wind direction.

Wind from direction D: The wind has hardly any influence on an increased perception of the cross track, the position of the steps is mainly decisive here.

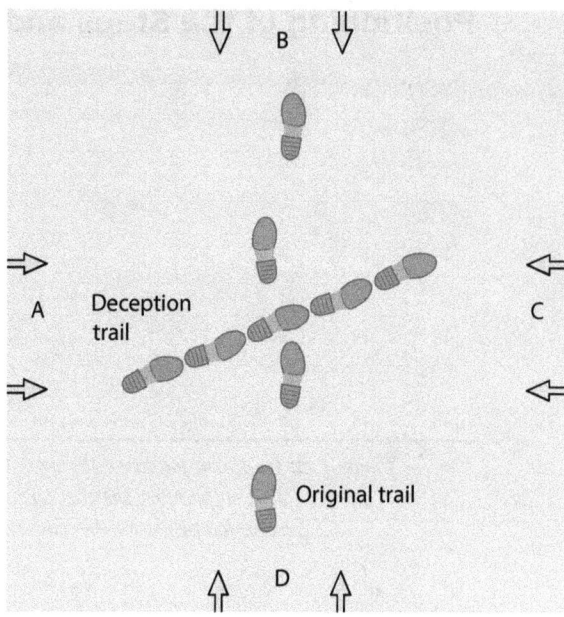

Perception of the cross track depending on the wind.

Different Degree of Decomposition of the Original Track and the Cross Track

Particularly tricky are the cross tracks that have a stronger smell than the original track. The stronger smell may be due to a more intensive gait or shorter paces. Or the original track has hardly any smell left due to environmental influences (heavy rain, high temperatures, frost, etc.) and the younger track is easier to smell. For example, if the original track was laid on frozen terrain and the cross track on defrosted terrain. It is then a great temptation for a dog that has difficulty finding the original track to switch to the easier-to-find cross track. Highly visible cross tracks are a great temptation for many dogs.

Things to Know

During training, old tracks frequently cross the original track. Keep in mind that these old tracks can also unsettle an inexperienced dog, or the dog may even switch to these tracks. Be prepared for this and correct in time.

Cross track training can unsettle dogs in their whole track behavior. Especially in the area of the corners, they initially no longer show confident track behavior. Therefore, lay the corners of the original track very carefully and possibly more easily than it corresponds to the training level of the dog. Have patience and lay easy tracks without any cross tracks in between until the track behavior has stabilized.

Besides a laid cross track, game tracks can tempt a dog to leave the track and follow the game spoor. Therefore, ignoring wild game tracks must be practiced as often as possible.

Faulty Associations of the Dog during Cross Track Training

The dog learns during cross track training which track he should follow and which not. He tries to distinguish between the original track and the cross track. He could, as desired, take the changed scent of the cross track in comparison to the original track as a distinguishing feature. But it could also be that he first chooses other distinguishing criteria. These could be:

- The different types (pace width, intensity of the ground violation, etc.), how the cross track was laid.

- The other individual scent that accompanies the cross track, if the cross track was laid by someone other than the original track layer.

- The design of the crossing. At the crossing point is a corner on the right and left of the track.

This dog is aware of the presence of a deceptive cross track but continues to track with confidence.

In order to identify the dog's faulty linkages:

- Always lay the cross track yourself at the beginning.
- Always lay the cross track differently.

Observe closely which cross tracks your dog wants to follow. How was the cross track laid, what is the time difference between the original track and the cross track, what is the current wind direction, who laid the cross track? Target training these cross tracks specifically.

Even many experienced dogs who have learned to confidently not accept a cross track always need a refresher on cross track training.

Example: Felix, an experienced tracking dog, ignores every cross track. He reliably tracks the original track and does not switch to the cross track, even if it is clearly visible. As a result, the dog handler unintentionally omits occasional cross track training. Of all things, the effects become apparent at important supra-regional trials. Felix switches to the cross track in two trials in a row. The consequence: Termination of the trial, failed! After a year of cross track training, he again ignores the cross tracks reliably and stays on the original track.

Case Study
Exercise Arrangement for All Wind Directions

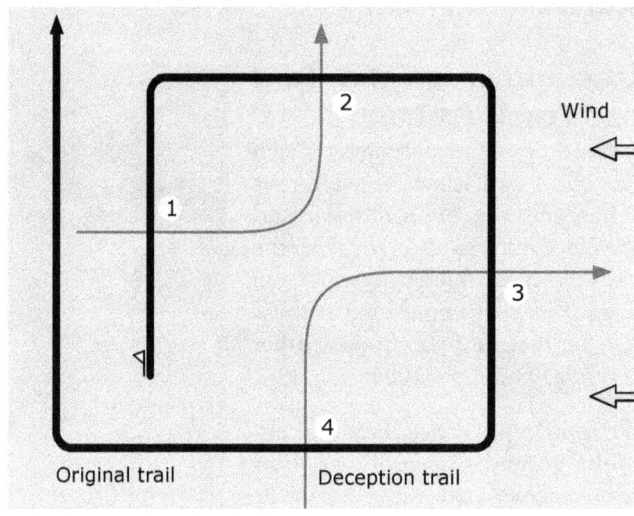

Example of cross track training. The thick black line is the track. The gray lines are the cross tracks.

The path to be tracked is labeled 1 and 4. The cross tracks are labeled 2 and 3.

Point 1: Wind comes from the right, the cross track approaching the original track from the right is more likely to be perceived than the cross track section to the left of the track.

Point 2: Wind is coming from the front, cross track is clearly perceived, both to the right and to the left of the track.

Point 3: Wind comes from the left, cross track to the left of the track is perceived more clearly than cross track to the right of the track.

Point 4: Wind comes from behind, cross track is hardly noticed.

The direction of laying the cross track most likely has very little effect on perceiving it. The influence of the wind on the perception of the cross track is probably much stronger than the direction of the cross track. That is, whether the cross track goes from point 3 to point 4, for example, or from point 4 to point 3.

Path Crossings

A track can lead over a path. How this should look is not further specified in the trial regulations. Mostly the track runs straight over the path. But also oblique courses occur. The path can be a field path, a meadow path, a gravel path, or a paved path. Again: All conceivable variations are to be trained little by little. The dog should try to follow the route of the track in the area of the path and not simply go to the other side of the path with a high nose and only continue the track work there.

Preparation and Implementation

As soon as the dog shows a confident track behavior in the area of straight lines and corners, a straight line can also lead over a path. In this case, the track should have food directly in front of the path, as well as in the direct area of the path and a short distance after it. The sequence of

A Straight Line Over
The track layer lays the training track; a straight line leads over a path. This can be asphalt or overgrown.

The track leads towards the path crossing.

The dog searches the path with a low nose.

Intensive tracking continues after crossing the path.

paces in the area of the path should be very easy to track, i.e., step behind step and no lateral offset. The food motivates the dog to track across the path, but still tracks because that is where he will find the food. The handler should always keep in mind that in the area of a path apart from the change of ground scent, many other scents can distract the dog, such as feces and urine of other dogs. The handler follows the dog a little closer right before crossing a path than during normal training. If the dog shows uncertainty, the handler helps by pointing gestures or the like.

123

If the dog knows the auditory signal "ahead," he can be sent across the path. However, the dog then does not learn to follow the scent of the track across the path with a deep nose.

For example, a male beagle works the training track that leads over a path for the first time. Right at the edge of the path he interrupts the track, lifts his leg and marks and then continues tracking. Everything happens so fast that the handler cannot react. At the next crossing of the path he is forewarned. He stops the marking with a clear "no," "search."

Ideal Behavior of the Dog on the Track

The dog follows the route of the track across the path with a deep nose and steady speed.

Undesirable Behavior of the Dog

Dog lifts head and stops tracking, dog gets distracted by scents on the path (e.g., marking scents of other dogs) and leaves the track, dog lifts head and goes to the other side of the track without tracking, dog does not change to the other side of the track, continues trying to find the track.

Intensive search at a path crossing.

From Easy to Difficult

A straight road crossing as shown in A is usually easier for the dog than an oblique course B of the track across the path. Strong crosswinds C also increase the difficulty of a trail crossing.

The condition of the trail edge (e.g., nettles, ditch, or similar) can also increase the difficulty of a trail crossing.

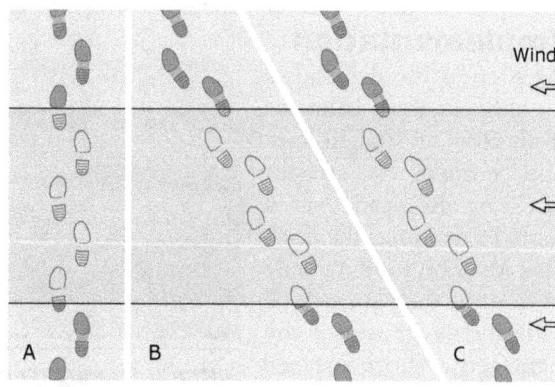

Different tracks over one trail.

The fewer natural components the road has, which can decompose, the more difficult it becomes for the dog to still perceive the scent of the track. Over a large asphalt road only the abrasion of the shoe on the road or the experience of the dog helps the dog to track.

Here you can practice many things: path crossings, animal crossings, different terrain, etc.

Difficulty Levels of a Track

This checklist is designed to help you assess the difficulty of a track in its entirety and in specific areas.

Example 1: Your dog reliably works the straight lines and also corners in soft damp ground. You want to increase the difficulty. You can now either choose a more difficult terrain to track or make the pace sequence more difficult (longer paces or a larger pace width) but not all at once. If there is unusually strong wind when you are laying your training track, keep the usual pace and terrain. The wind already increases the difficulty of the track sufficiently.

If your dog does not show the ideal track behavior, you should determine the reasons. This list will also help you to do this.

Example 2: Your dog does not consistently track a corner. He stops and needs your help. However, the corner is laid in the same way as the previous ones he consistently tracked. On the basis of the list, you could suspect the following reasons for his behavior: the wind comes at this corner from a direction unfavorable for the track, the corner lies in another terrain, the corner lies directly on a tractor track, etc. Depending on your guess, you should train this situation more.

Here is a selection of the most important factors influencing the difficulty of a track:

- Soil characteristics of the terrain (soft, hard, loamy, sandy, etc.)
- Terrain vegetation
- Wind force, wind direction
- Air and soil moisture (rain, drought, showers)
- Temperature (heat, frost, mild temperatures)
- Environment of the tracking area (forest, game, paths, people, etc.)
- Step intensity
- Pace length
- Pace width
- Pace direction
- Direction of the track in relation to terrain structures (tractor tracks, seed lines, etc.)
- Design of the corners (radius or right corner)
- Size of the corner (right-cornered, acute, obtuse)
- Design of the semicircle
- Material, frequency of use (new, often used), length of time worn on the track layer's body, stranger's articles
- Own track, strange track
- Location of the articles
- Design of the terrain changes
- Design of the cross track
- Track length

Each of these factors affects the difficulty of a track. They also influence each other. Strong wind influences the difficulty of, among other things, a straight line and a corner as well as a trail crossing.

Reminder:
Always adapt the training track to your dog's level of training. For example, if you consider the terrain very difficult to track and your dog cannot yet track all levels of difficulty, design your pace length and width and the intensity of your step in a way to help the dog find the track. If you want to increase the difficulty of individual factors of a training track, do this in the middle part of the track. The dog can then track the initial part of the track consistently, in the middle part he may have difficulties, and at the end he can again show a confident track.

Keep Practicing

Here you can practice many things – path crossing, game crossing, variable terrains, etc.

Which difficulties are you likely to be able to train in particular in able to train in particular in a field like the one shown on the right. Consider track length, oblique and vertical seed furrows, high and low vegetation growth, meadow and field, change of terrain, game tracks, change of wind impact (following shrubs, at the edge of the terrain), slight slope, corner in tractor track, proximity to path behind shrubs (possible smell of dog feces and urine, distraction through walkers).

What can you train here?

Fitness

For track work, a dog needs good physical fitness and a strong ability to concentrate. Both must be trained. Let us review once again. Intensive smelling during track work is a different process than normal breathing to oxygenate the animal. In stressful environmental conditions such as heat, sniffing breathing competes with vital breathing. A strong basic fitness of the dog is therefore important. This causes the dog not to start panting quickly during physical exertion at normal outside temperatures. This basic fitness condition of the dog should be trained outside the tracking work. In particular, interval training strengthens the general heart and lung function. Likewise, muscles that are used because of the search posture and during sniffing breathing must be built up, as well as the dog's ability to concentrate.

Depending on the dog's individual disposition, training can be done several times a week (in relatively short sessions) or just once a week. Watch your dog closely for the first signs of demotivation such as frequent high nose, stopping, unwillingness to approach or leave the car before training. It often helps to take a break with training so that eventually you can start again with new pizzazz.

Adjust the length and difficulty of your training tracks to your dog. Train shorter training tracks more often and very long tracks less often (>1800 paces for IGP-FH training).

Do not increase all the difficulty factors of the training track at the same time. When you start

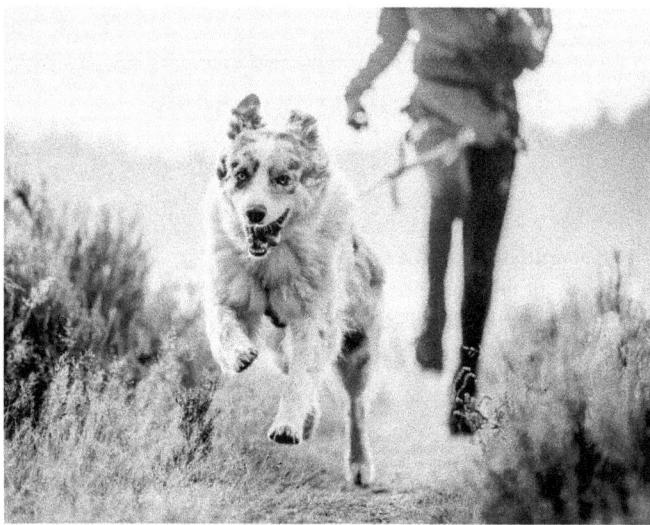

Jogging or cycling with your dog can help you build up his fitness.

training longer tracks, design easy ones at first. And if you already know when laying the track that it will be quite difficult to track, this training track should not be too long for a not fully trained dog. You can see what is too long by your dog's behavior: He will lift his head more often, maybe the nose is not as far down, the body tension decreases and possibly the tail drops significantly. If your dog's undesirable behavior accumulates during a long track, end the track early with a positive experience for your dog while tracking. The next article that the dog indicates is suitable for this. In doing so, he will be rewarded by the handler. If you have to stop the track quickly because the dog is very exhausted, throw food on the track, as unnoticed by the dog as possible. As soon as he picks up the food, stop the track.

If you want your dog to continue tracking despite severe signs of fatigue, your dog may become accustomed to less than intense tracking behavior and you may have to correct him often during the track work. This would then demotivate the dog in addition to his exhaustion.

Short Leash-Long Leash

If you use a leash to lead your dog in tracking work (the normal case), adjust the leash length and thus the distance to the dog, to the training objective.

For normal training, a 2 to 3 meter/6 to10 feet distance from the dog works well. You must be able to watch your dog closely at all times and correct him, e.g., by blocking the leash. This allows you to see the route of the track more easily. You will also be able to see whether your dog picks up all the food or not. Only when your dog tracks reliably and consistently, can you leave the leash longer in easy passages of the track - but only if you know the position of the corners, the articles, and the straight lines with certainty from a distance of 10 meters/33 feet.

Handler follows at 6 to 10 feet behind the dog.

Proper way to hold the leash so that it does not slip from your hand.

Trial regulations stipulate a 10 meter/33 feet distance from the dog. So you must train this distance. Many dogs are initially unsettled by the greater distance, especially at the corners. Therefore, increase the distance to the dog only when your dog is confident in the tracking work.

Loose or Taut

Whether your dog should track on a loose or taut leash depends on your dog and you. Does your dog have too fast a search speed? Does he need the security that a taut leash gives him by connecting him to you? Depending on the breed of dog, the dog's personality and the corrective action needed, a taut or loose leash may be appropriate. Impulsive hunting dogs will be difficult to train to track very calmly on a loose leash without robbing them of the joy of tracking.

Handling in Corners

At 90° corners, the handler must walk an arc to keep the leash taut and/or not snag on bumps or plants in the terrain and then block the dog.

Taut leash control is not possible at acute corners. Some dogs, therefore, tend to accelerate after the corner. This behavior should be prevented by a suitable design of the track from the beginning. Because the leash drags on the ground in this area, it can get caught in the terrain. The leash then blocks briefly and the dog must get it free. He may have to get used to this unintentional jerking of the leash.

It also happens from time to time that the dog circles on the track, causing the leash to wrap around a leg, for example. Do not intervene at first. The dog should be able to free himself. If he cannot do this, help him. However, during trial do this only with prior permission from the judge.

Many handlers tend to let the leash slip through their hand more and more during tracking work, thereby imperceptibly increasing the distance to the dog. This makes corrections more difficult. Hold the leash firmly in your hand.

Solving Behavior Problems

Solving problems has to be learned. And problems come up again and again in tracking training both for the dog and for the handler.

In this context, problems are usually indications of training mistakes or deficits.

Let's deal with it accordingly and not blame our dog. We, as dog handlers, are responsible for teaching our dog to work a track according to his abilities. The dog must also learn to deal with problems that arise. He should solve them independently, but within the framework of the correct track behavior.

What the handler sees as a problem is stress for most dogs, sometimes caused only by the handler's reaction. It depends on the dog how strongly he perceives this stress and reacts to it. In tracking training, the following situations, among others, can be problematic for the dog: he can no longer find the track, he gets caught in the leash, he is in an inner conflict between what he should do and what he wants to do at the moment. For example, if a tracking dog (e.g., a terrier) smells game in the headwind, he actually prefers to follow the game scent. However, he knows that he is supposed to track the scent of footsteps. This conflict puts the dog under stress.

Ideal Problem Solving Behavior

If a problem arises while working the track, the dog should stay on the track and only continue when he finds the route of the track. He can use his nose to the right and left of the track to track the further route of the track, but he should not leave the track with his body. When learning a suitable problem-solving behavior, the handler's sure instinct is required.

Some dogs get frantic when problems arise and start running and jumping around. Some put their heads up and sniff the wind. Others look to the handler for help, turn to him, and seek eye contact. Some act as if they have no problem and just keep tracking. Again, the training must suit your dog. For example, a dog that is not independent must be encouraged to find a solution on his own, initially with the help of the handler. Support your dog with pointing gestures, praise or similar. In any case, do not leave your dog helpless.

If your dog is rather uncontrollably trying to find the scent by unsystematic movements, limit his range of movement by the leash and try to calm him down (e.g., by a calm voice).

What problem-solving behavior is achievable for your dog depends, among other things, on your dog's temperament and personality. For some dogs, it is difficult enough not to become hyper-excited when a problem arises. In this case, it is already a great training success if the dog tracks around slowly with a low nose when a problem arises and tries to solve the problem.

Each dog has his own behavior to solve problems. Therefore, you will find suggestions for correction of a wide variety of behaviors in the following chart.

Problem solving behavior

Typical Problem Solving Behavior	Sensible Responses
Dog stops, lifts head and stands indecisively	Auditory signal "search" (if already conditioned) may help, possibly accompanied by a pointing gesture
Dog stops and turns to handler	Encouragement (by motivating voice), auditory signal "search," may possibly help, sometimes it is useful to wait first
Dog starts walking around slowly with deep nose tracking	Let the dog work, do not interfere, possibly restrict the radius by blocking the leash
Dog lies down	Support the dog with pointing gestures, watch for fear or calming signals, encourage fear-free training!!!
Dog stops and tries to solve the problem by movements of the head with deep nose	Praise
Avoidance behavior (eating grass or rabbit droppings)	Auditory signal "search," friendly voice, do not build up further stress
Dog stops tracking	Motivate
Dog running around frantically tracking	Calming, helping with pointing gestures, restricting range of movement by shortening and blocking the leash, use impulse control training
Dog tries to solve problem, but then stops tracking	Encourage dog, help if necessary, do not leave dog standing helplessly
Growling, avoidance behavior, calming signals, "freezing of movement": behaviors of a dog that perceives a problem, or the handler's reaction to a situation, as a threat. These behaviors are also known in literature as fight, flight, flirt, freeze	Reconsider type of training, dog should not perceive any phase of tracking training as a threat

4. The Training Track

Knowing How and Where

Note: At this point of the book we will move forward to working on actual training tracks where you can apply what you have learned in the previous chapters. You will also learn here what you would need to know if you choose to compete in organized tracking trials.

Knowing the Route of the Track

Most training mistakes happen because the handler does not remember the exact route of the track. When the handler does not know where the track is, he won't know if his dog is exactly on the track. Therefore, he cannot correct the dog if necessary or recognize his dog's training level. If, for example, a dog walks over most corners during a trial, then tracks back and forth, and finds the next straight line after a while and continues tracking, the undesirable behavior might be inaccurate training. This behavior can happen if the dog handler does not recognize during training why his dog is, for example, overwhelmed with the difficulty of a corner. Because he does not remember the exact location of the corner, he cannot analyze why his dog does not exactly track the corner. Of course, there could also be other reasons for the described behavior but the most frequent problem is the dog handler who does not remember exactly where the track is. And exactly means +/- one hand's width.

As a dog handler, you need to know the following for tracking training:

- The beginning of the track (marked by scent pad marker)
- The course of straight lines
- The position of the corners
- The course of the semicircles
- The location of the articles and
- Where you change the pace width, pace length or the intensity of the steps in sections of the track

An item is placed on the training track in a field with low vegetation.

Natural Points of Orientation

To remember these points, orient yourself to conspicuous points in the terrain. Some points are more suitable as orientation aids, some less. The following table gives you an overview of the use of different landmarks.

Retrieval of...	Orientation through...
Beginning of the track	Scent pad marker
Direction of a straight line	Conspicuous points in the distant surroundings (wind turbines, church tower, crossroads, posts, etc.) Conspicuous points in the terrain (tufts of grass, flowers, change of vegetation, tractor tracks, stones, etc.)
Position of the corner, articles, semicircle	Conspicuous points near the track (tufts of grass, flowers, change of vegetation, tractor tracks, stones, change of terrain, etc.) Counting paces to the corner, articles etc. This is sometimes the only way to remember the location of a corner or article. Unsuitable for accurate orientation: the imaginary extension of more distant landmarks, this is too inaccurate.

The following is imperative: When working the track, the handler is 2 to 10 meters / 6 to 32 feet behind the dog. Even from this position, he should know exactly the route of the track. Not all landmarks that the dog handler perceives when laying the track can be recognized from this distance.

Using Aids

Recalling the details of the laid track needs a lot of practice and experience. There are aids that give the handler security in the beginning and allow good training of the dog. However, only use these if orientation in the terrain causes you great difficulty. Because every aid reduces one's own learning success since the attention is then more on the aids and no longer on remembering the orientation points in the terrain.

Different Aids and Their Advantages and Disadvantages.

Aid	Suitable for	Disadvantages
Tracking chalk for spraying	Marking of approximate direction and position of articles and corners possible	Is not supposed to smell, some dogs perceive it anyway Marking is only visible in a small radius
Tracking app	Allows a good overview of the route of the track Suitable for later documentation of the track	Distracts the handler's attention very much from the dog Accurate observation of the dog hardly possible Shows the route of the track only very inaccurately
Wooden sticks		Are often perceived by the dog and the danger of false conditioning is very high, observe whether your dog perceives the sticks Danger of injury Remove ALL sticks from the terrain after training
When laying the track you can take and place leaves, corn stalks, stones, etc.	Precise marking of corners and articles possible	Are often perceived by the dog and the danger of false conditioning is very high
Aluminum / metal rods NEVER LEAVE UNATTENDED IN THE FIELD A tractor tire can easily break if it runs over a metal rod!	Precise marking of corners and articles possible	Are perceived by the dog less than wooden sticks and the danger of false conditioning is not quite so great. Observe whether your dog perceives the rods Danger of injury BE SURE TO REMOVE ALL RODS

Use of Tracking Chalk

Tracking chalk is sprayed on the ground. Usually you can not see it from about 3m/10 feet. Therefore, when marking a corner, for example, you should mark the spot on the track where you will be standing when your dog will be at the corner. If your training distance to the dog is about 2m/6 feet, you should place the auxiliary marker 2m/6ft in front of the corner.

Use of Rods

Many dogs notice the rods even if they are not directly on the track. They are useful only in exceptional cases. If a handler cannot remember the course of a track at all, even after several months of practice, markers can be of help. They should be put as much to the side of the track as possible. NEVER leave metal rods unattended in terrain.

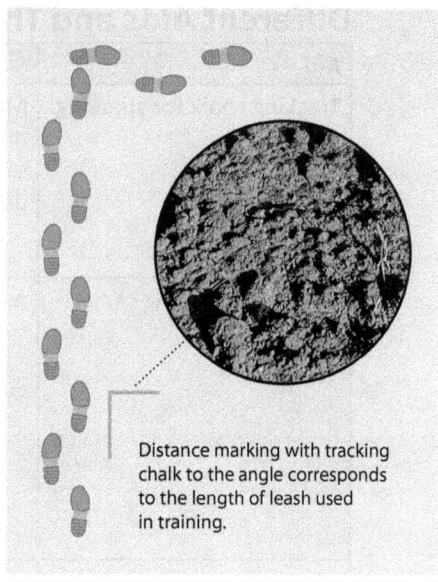

Distance marking with tracking chalk to the angle corresponds to the length of leash used in training.

Marking with track chalk.

Use of Natural Objects

You must always expect that your dog will perceive the landmarks such as branches, stones, etc. and associate them with the corner, etc. Therefore, vary the location of your landmarks. If you always place a corner directly at a tuft of grass or a stone, an attentive dog may associate tufts of grass with corners and look for corners at tufts of grass in general. "1m/3 feet in front of the tuft of grass" or "0.5m/1 ½ feet after the large stone" can also serve as orientation. Or you can, for example, place a stone next to the track from time to time, which has no significance for the route of the track.

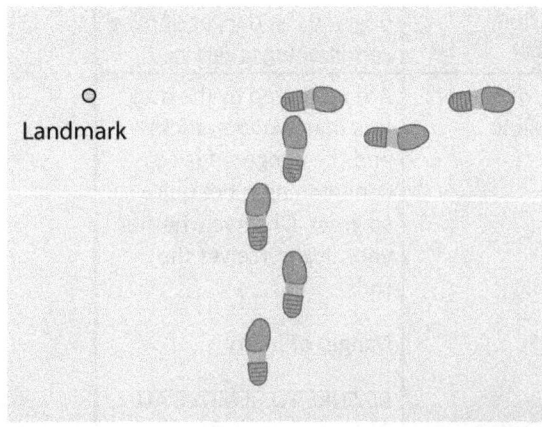

○
Landmark

Corner to the right, stick is to the left.

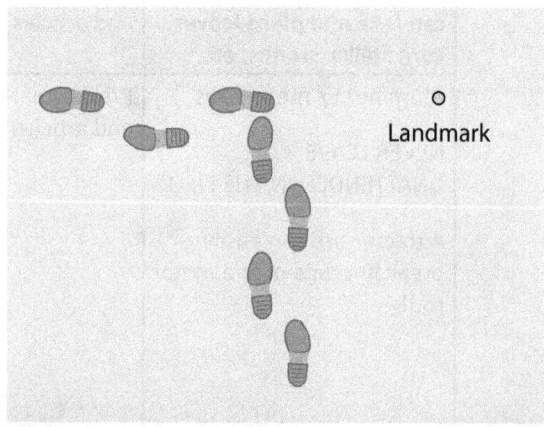

○
Landmark

Corner to the left, stick is to the right.

Landmarks in the field that help the handler know the exact route of the track should not be able to be associated with the track by the dog.

Do not change your landmarks while you are laying the track. Remember the first point you choose as an aid to orientation for the location of a corner, etc., even if you notice a more suitable landmark shortly thereafter. When working the track with your dog, you will usually spontaneously remember only your first landmark.

Tracking Diary

With a long track, you have to remember a lot of landmarks. For many handlers, it is helpful to write down the route of the track and the landmarks (track diary, track sketch).

Also, note time of day, wind direction, difficulties observed, and planned consequences for the next training track.

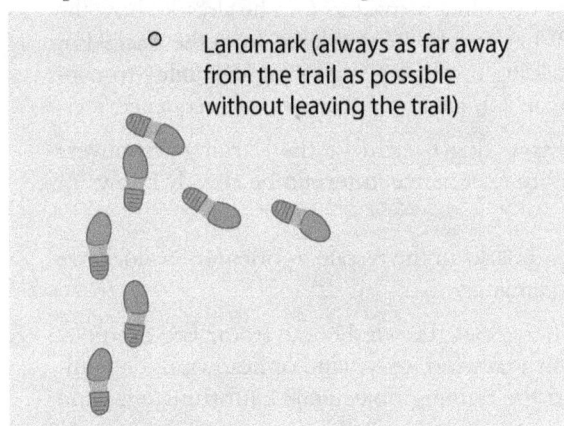

o Landmark (always as far away from the trail as possible without leaving the trail)

Acute angle, rod as far as possible straight ahead.

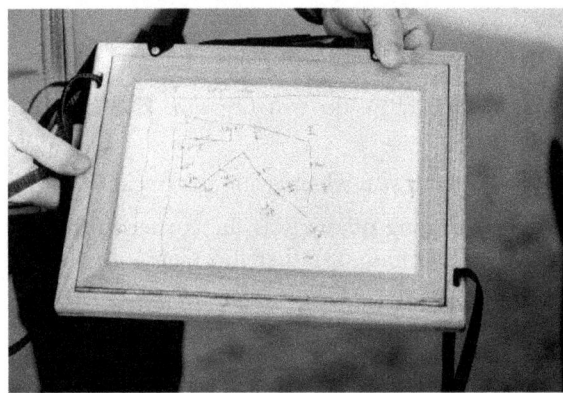

Corner to the left, rod is to the right.

Marking stick (always as far away from the track as possible without leaving the track).

Alternatively, you can also lay a track and then walk this track again without the dog. Can you find the exact route of the track with the help of your notes? Of course, this track is then no longer suitable for tracking training.

If you sketch and write down your tracks, you will also more easily recognize which unconscious regularities you have when laying tracks. Do you lay the track mostly with the first corner to the right or to the left? Where do the articles lie? All regularities when laying tracks can lead to false conditioning in the dog. For example, if an article always lies on the first straight line during training, a dog may become confused at the first corner when this article is missing.

> **Track Sketch**
> Draw your track with all landmarks. Give this sketch to a helper who will accompany you while you track with your dog. While your dog works the track, the helper reads the landmarks to you in advance. Can you and the helper accurately predict the route of the track from the sketch? If not, change the nature of your landmarks.

What to Consider When Track Laying:

- What terrain is available? Is a track likely to be difficult to track (such as dry vegetation, loamy-hard or sandy-fine-crumbly)?

- What was the dog's behavior during the last training track and what consequences to draw for the next training track?

- What level of difficulties can the dog already master? Can he already show the desired behavior consistently? What should the dog learn from the track? For example, confident tracking, building up fitness, increasing the ability to concentrate, increasing the difficulty in sub-areas, e.g., corner, pace sequence, etc.

- What terrain do you need for your dog to achieve the learning objectives? For example, should he gain more experience in terrain he already knows or learn new terrain?

- Are there likely to be enough landmarks in the terrain as orientation aids? Are aids needed to find the track again later?

- How strong is the wind and where does the wind come from? For example, should the first straight line be in a tailwind, crosswind or headwind (depending on the level of training and the training objective)? Unfortunately, wind conditions often change.

- What distractions are likely to exist such as proximity to forest game tracks and game smell, path with people and dogs, cows, wind turbines, power lines, etc.?

- Is your dog rested and healthy?

- How much time do you have available? How do you organize the time between laying and working the track?

- Do you have suitable treats and articles with you when laying the track?

- The course of the last training tracks (among others: was the corner to the right or left, was the first straight line rather long or rather short, etc.). Avoid the same courses of training tracks.

How Difficult Should a Track Be?

The training track needs to be adapted to the dog's level of training. And again, since this is often not considered, the first third of a normal training track should be easy for the dog, so that he can take up the track without problems and show intensive track behavior. If you want to increase the difficulty of the track, do so in the second third of the track. The last third of the track should be easy again for the dog.

Remember: one of the most important training objectives is a confident, joyful, and motivated track behavior. You should allow your dog to do this at least at the beginning and end of the track. Of course, there are exceptions. For example, if a dog is only superficially tracking the starting point, you can make the starting point more difficult for the dog. For example, lead the dog to the start from the side. This forces the dog to track more intensively and with greater concentration. Of course, you can also lay a challenging starting point for an experienced dog from time to time.

After these preliminary considerations, lay the training track and memorize its course well.

The quality of the training track (appropriate to the dog's level of training and easy for the handler to find again) determines to a large extent the learning success of your dog.

Having Someone Else Lay the Track

If you have another dog handler lay a training track for you, he should also observe all the points mentioned. Laying a track without knowing the dog's training level and an exact training objective can only help to roughly check the training level and then only if the track layer can always tell the handler whether the dog is exactly on the track. If he cannot do this, lay the training track yourself. However, if you know an experienced track layer, have him lay a track for you from time to time. Some dogs react confused to a track laid by someone else.

And when you lay the track, use things you see on it: Boar scat, rabbit droppings, discarded articles, and more. Lay the track directly over them or at a short distance from them, so that your dog learns to ignore these things.

Satisfied after the track: This dog was obviously searching in the field with his nose deep in the ground.

On the Training Track

The training track is laid. After 20 minutes at the earliest (or up to 3 hours later, depending on the training objective), the handler and his dog get ready for the track work. He walks his dog and lets him urinate and defecate. He does warm-up exercises with his dog. He makes sure that his dog is not thirsty and that he has enough treats. He recalls the route of the track.

A dog handler needs: time, patience, a clear idea of correct track behavior, good observation skills, and good memory.

Simultaneously during training, you need to:

- Identify the exact route of the track
- Observe the behavior of your dog
- Choose the right distance to your dog (this can change during the route of the track)
- Possibly control the search speed of your dog
- Observe the wind direction (for the undesirable behavior analysis)
- If necessary, correct, praise or reprimand your dog, and
- Keep an eye on the near and far surroundings of the track (stray dogs, rabbits in the field, etc.)

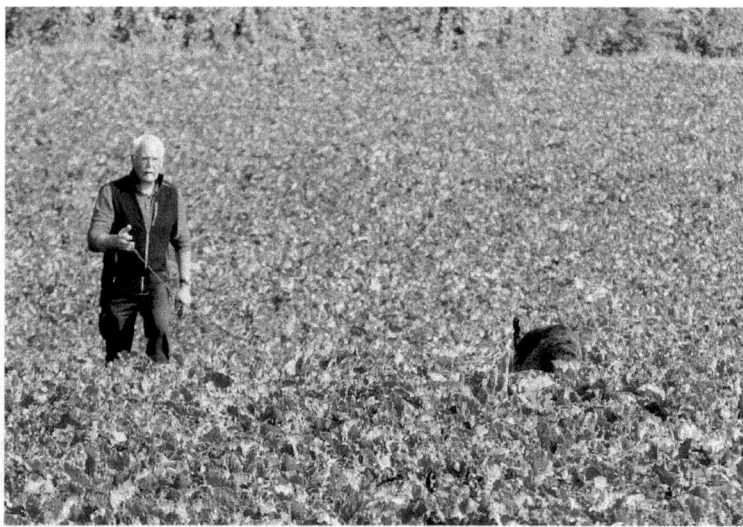

Here it is a challenge to know the route of the trail.

Training at any time of the year, here in summer.

Practice Makes Perfect

If possible, have experienced dog handlers accompany you and exchange your observations. Otherwise, mistakes in training will creep in unnoticed and will be difficult to correct, if at all.

The most common reasons for a dog showing undesirable behaviors in training are an unsuitable training track and incorrect evaluations of the dog's demonstrated behavior (e.g., "He doesn't feel like it today; he already knows what to do") instead of correct observations. Unfortunately, sometimes these inappropriate evaluations are then used as the basis for corrective measures that are not sensible.

Focus and Teamwork

Working a training track requires the handler's full attention. Track work is teamwork and many dogs also react to an inattentive handler by losing their own concentration.

After the track work, praise your dog extensively. Do stretching exercises with him. Take him for a short walk and give him water.

After the track work, consider where the dog exhibited ideal track behavior and where he showed undesirable behavior on the training track. Consider possible reasons for his behavior. You will always need to know the wind direction affecting the track. Plan your next training track so that your dog is not likely to show the same undesirable behavior.

Pitfalls When Laying a Track

Every dog handler has preferences on how he lays the track. It may be that he almost always lays the first corner to the right, or the starting point is always at a great distance from a path. In training, your dog should be prepared for tracks that are laid by another handler. The handler will lay the track differently than you. Therefore, during training, you must repeatedly lay the training track contrary to your own habits. Think about the following questions and get to know your own habits when laying a track.

Tracking is a challenge for your fitness, memory and sense of balance.

Questionnaire for Detecting Unconscious Regularities in Tracking

- Does your first corner lead to the right or to the left? Is it a 90° corner or an acute one?

- Where do you put the treats and at what intervals? In the left or right shoe prints, front or back, regularly, etc.?

- Is your design of the steps always the same (intensity, pace width, etc.)?

- Does your track always have the same distances to terrain edges, paths, or streets?

- In which direction and how do your straight lines run? Are they always along terrain lines (seed furrows, machining furrows), or only oblique to them, or in elongated serpentine lines?

- Where do you place articles? In the shoe print in front, behind, or in between; across, oblique, or toward the track?

- Where do you put corners? In the middle of the terrain or always close to the terrain change or path?

- How do you lay corners? With or without radius? Do you change your pace before or after?

- Do you always place a corner before, after, or directly at a prominent point in the terrain?

But even if you want to avoid regularities, you need to know exactly where the track is. Increase the difficulty only when the dog is consistently tracking the previous tracks. Use treats intentionally to support the learning process.

The food is placed in each step at the beginning, later more irregularly and sometimes at the front, sometimes at the back.

Intensive search...

...brief lifting of the head...

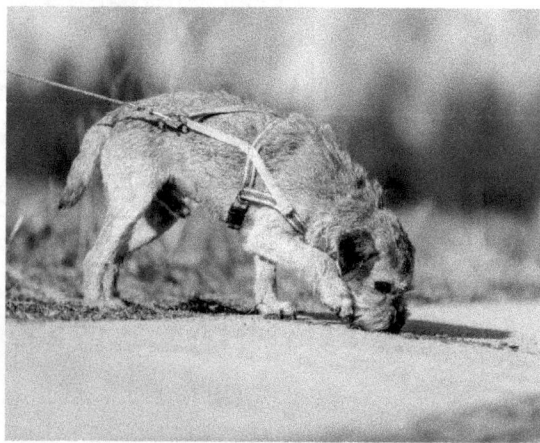

...very intensive search for a route.

5. Troubleshooting

*Corrections, Planning,
Observing, Reacting*

Between Planning and Correcting

In addition to the individual abilities of the dog, two factors are decisive for the success of tracking training: suitable training tracks and appropriate rewards and corrections. Planning and laying the training track were the topics of the previous chapters. This chapter is about the interaction between dog and handler. If the dog shows the desired behavior, he is praised. If the dog shows an undesirable behavior, what can a sensible reaction of the handler to troubleshoot the problem look like? Which corrections are useful? If the training structure is right and the dog is challenged according to his performance level, usually only minor corrections are necessary. Praise your dog! Show him when he did something right. He cannot know on his own what you want from him. Praise him again and again when he does something right. Correction is everything that the handler shows in his reactions when the dog shows an undesirable behavior, i.e., from an unwilling noise, to a helping pointing gesture, to blocking the leash. Sometimes a corrective measure is also a change in the design of the next training track.

If you skipped some of the previous chapters, here's a quick summary of the principles for a good training setup.

Principles of Training Planning

Plan your training track so that your dog is likely to track without too much difficulty. It is better to have a very easy track than a track that is too difficult. The dog should show confident track behavior on the track. He learns this best with training tracks that are not too difficult for him. If a dog is constantly overtaxed, he tends to browse more than track. He then shows a behavior in which he constantly sniffs to the right and left of the track and does not follow the track purposefully. He finds the track but does not show the desired track behavior.

Some things are easier to correct with two people.

Have Patience in Training

One of the most common mistakes in training is increasing the difficulty of the track too quickly. Always make sure your dog understands what you want. This is easier said than done. Before you get angry about your dog's undesirable behavior, consider whether your dog knows that you don't want the shown behavior. Give your dog time to learn. When learning, your dog goes through several learning phases. These are:

- Learn new behavior
- Show new behavior
- Show new behavior under different conditions
- Show new behavior all the time

This means: If your dog shows the desired behavior a few times, e.g., with a suitable aid, do not immediately remove these aids. Otherwise, incorrect behavior will quickly become apparent, which then has to be tediously corrected again.

And very important: You need an idea of what correct track work looks like and an exact knowledge of the track route. You will find a description of the respective ideal track behavior in Chapter 3: Training Structure: Step by Step.

When It Does Not Go Smoothly

And despite all the good preparation, the dog sometimes shows behavior during training that is not desired by the handler. What can the handler do then? First, carefully observe your dog and the situation, then determine the presumed reasons for the behavior, and only then possibly correct the dog. Observe-Interpret-React: This procedure must be carried out very quickly during training.

Correcting essentially means making clear to the dog what the handler expects of him in terms of behavior. The tables in this book also follow this procedure. First, the observed behavior is described, the influencing factors are named and interpretations are made as to why the dog shows the respective undesirable behavior. Depending on the interpretation, corrective measures are suggested. If the handler carries out the suggested corrections, and the dog then shows the desired behavior (sometimes only after a certain period of adjustment), this confirms the underlying interpretation. If the correction has no positive effect on the track behavior, other reasons for the undesirable behavior must be assumed and the training adapted accordingly.

For example: The dog repeatedly lifts his head on a straight line and looks around. You look for the table "Dog Lifts Nose or Head" on page 155. There you will find under "lifts head and looks around" further considerations about the probable causes and suitable corrections.

The corrections are tried and tested in practice but can of course be varied depending on the situation, the dog, and the handler. When developing new corrections yourself, always consider how the exercise looks from the dog's point of view and whether it can teach him what you want.

It is often underestimated how extensive the task of the dog handler is during training, which is hidden behind these terms Observe-Interpret-React (Correct/Reward). Here is a brief summary of the most important aspects of these terms.

The article is under the dog's chest.

The dog's nose is not close enough to the ground.

Restless impetuous tracking with nose high.

Very intensive with a low nose and a high tail.

Observe

When observing, it is important that you first only observe your dog and the overall situation. The second step is the interpretation of the observation.

Example: Indicating an article. A dog handler is annoyed because his dog only unwillingly indicates an article. But "unwillingly" is not an observation but an interpretation of what the handler sees. Probably he observed his dog indicate the article very slowly. If he immediately concludes that the dog is unwilling to indicate, without further observation this may lead to inappropriate training measures. The slow indicating can have many causes, among other things: uncertainty because it is the first time using an article which smells of another person (stranger`s article), a physical overtaxing of the dog by the track, another position of the article than the dog is used to, unaccustomed material of the article and more. But here we are already in the area of interpretation.

As a handler, keep the following in mind during training:
- **The body language of your dog and his behavior.** The posture of the tail, the ears, the trunk, the head, the nose, sounds heard when the dog inhales and exhales, the overall impression of the dog (state of arousal, body tension, panting, drooling, etc.), pulling on the leash, speed when tracking, distance of the nose to the track, etc.
- **The design of the track.** Sequence of paces, design of the corner, route of the track in relation to the surrounding ground (tractor tracks, vegetation, length of the track, etc.).
- **Environmental conditions.** Wind direction and force, dryness, wetness, frost, solar radiation, heat, etc.

Interpret

For successful training, the handler must understand his dog and his behavior. To do this, he must be able to observe and interpret the dog's body language on the track and the training factors (wind, temperature, pacing, etc.) in detail. However, he should always keep in mind that his thoughts about the reasons for his dog's behavior are only guesses. He must verify them through further training and correct them if necessary.

If the dog handler in the example described above is of the opinion that a stranger's articles are the reason for the slow indicating of his dog, the dog would have to point faster with his own articles. If he does not do that, the interpretation was wrong and new considerations are necessary. If the dog shows slow indicating, for example, with wooden articles, he might be unsure if he is supposed to indicate an article made of wood at all. For him, this might not be considered an article.

Respond and/or Correct

Let's get this straight right off the bat: The most common reaction to an undesirable behavior of a dog in training is to change the design of the next training track. And during the actual training, the handler standing still and blocking the leash, sometimes combined with an abort auditory signal. "No," is usually the most appropriate reaction.

In addition to these corrective measures, however, the handler has many more possibilities at his disposal to respond to (correct) his dog's behavior. These can be:

- Praise and reprimand with the help of the voice, different forms of expression possible, "Great," unwilling sound of the handler
- Stopping the track
- Pointing gestures
- Auditory signals, "Down," "Search," etc.
- Change the food or treats

In order for the dog to obey even quiet auditory signals, the dog should generally respond to corrections from the handler, not just on the track. This requires continuous training outside of tracking work as well.

In this book, the auditory signal "No" is used as a termination auditory signal. When it is given, the dog should stop his behavior. However, the handler must immediately make it clear to the dog what he expects from him instead of the undesirable behavior. In tracking training, a "No" is usually followed by a "Search." "Search" means: the dog should track intensively with a deep nose. Like every auditory signal, the dog must first learn the meaning of "Search" and master it. Only then can the dog understand what alternative behavior the handler expects from him.

Which Corrections Are Useful?
The only reasonable answer is that it depends on the dog and handler.

Since dogs of different breeds and origins now are used to track, the training method, including the type of corrections, must be adapted to each dog. Very self-confident dogs must be taught early on by the handler to track and work very accurately. With insecure, hesitant dogs, on the other hand, you may need to tolerate inaccuracies at times so that the dog does not become even more insecure. This balancing between correcting and temporarily not correcting, letting the dog solve problems on his own and helping him, is the art of successful tracking training.

What is useful and helpful for one dog in terms of correction by the handler may have the opposite training effect on another dog. The motto here is certainly: Trial and error. In dog training, no one is born a master. The dog handler learns together with his dog.

Responding Quickly
When a handler wants to correct his dog, he must do so in a very tight time frame. There should be no more than two seconds between behavior and correction so the dog can make an association between his behavior and the correction. Otherwise, it can happen that the dog does not correctly relate the corrective measure to the undesirable behavior just shown. This temporal relationship is generally important when praising and reprimanding the dog. For example, if a handler wants to signal to his dog that his track behavior is just right, and he waits too long with the praise, the dog will lift his head just at the moment of praise. And it has already happened: The wrong behavior has been praised. A similar risk exists if the dog handler does not exactly know the route of the track. Perhaps the dog is tracking two hand widths off the track and the handler has not noticed this and praises the dog at just the wrong time.

The dog handler must constantly make decisions during training as to whether and when to intervene, praise, or reprimand. Depending on the training situation, a reprimand can be useful for the one dog in this situation and for the same dog, on the next occasion, a reprimand is counterproductive. It is impossible to avoid making mistakes. Therefore, observe your dog's reactions closely.

For example, a dog leaves the track while tracking and works about 20 cm/8 inches beside the track. To correct or not? Assuming the presumed reason for the behavior is a game spoor that he wants to investigate: then a correction by a reprimand makes sense. If the handler does not reprimand his dog in this situation, he will presumably continue to follow game tracks.

However, if the reason for the dog's behavior is a very difficult track, then the handler should rather encourage his dog to continue tracking intensively. If he reprimands his dog when he does not find a track, this unsettles the dog because he is concentrating intensely on his work.

If the handler has decided to reprimand in this situation and the dog immediately returns exactly to the track, the interpretation of a distraction was correct. If he does not return, the track is either too difficult or the dog usually does not react to reprimands anyway.

Decisions and Their Consequences

A small number of the possible consequences of a decision during training are shown in the following figures. Depending on the dog, other consequences are conceivable.

CORRECT

Positive Consequences	Negative Consequences
Gives security	Unsettles
Encourages more precise behavior	Encourages avoidance behavior
Promotes learning process	Distracts
	Makes dependent

DO NOT CORRECT

Positive Consequences	Negative Consequences
Promotes learning process	Unsettles
Promotes independent tracking	Hinders learning process
	Promotes undesirable track behavior (e.g., rummaging)

PRAISE

Positive Consequences	Negative Consequences
Provides security	Distracts
Motivates	Hinders the learning process
Promotes the learning process	Promotes undesirable track behavior (e.g., rummaging)
	Superficial tracking

REPRIMANDING

Positive Consequences	Negative Consequences
Encourages more precise behavior	Unsettles
Increases concentration	Encourages avoidance behavior
Promotes learning process	De-motivates

TREATS ON TRACK

Positive Consequences	Negative Consequences
Gives security	Distracts
Encourages more precise behavior	Hinders learning process
Intensive tracking, deep nose	Encourages undesirable track behavior (e.g., rummaging)
Increases concentration	
Promotes the learning process	
Motivates	
Nose in every step	

NO TREATS ON TRACK

Positive Consequences	Negative Consequences
Promotes learning process	De-motivates
Encourages independent tracking	Encourages unwanted tracking behavior (e.g., rummaging)
	Superficial tracking

In the following tables, you will find tips for the handler's reaction on the track under **A** and suggestions for laying the next training track under **B**. For some undesirable behaviors in track behavior you will only find suggestions under **A** or **B** . This is intentional.

In the tables, you will first find the most obvious undesirable behavior as the heading. In the individual columns of the table, this undesirable behavior is supplemented by further factors. Only then do you find a column with the interpretations about the reasons for the undesirable behavior, and the last column describes corrective measures. And then there are behaviors of a dog that are out of the ordinary. In the middle of tracking, a dog begins to eat or shake himself even though his fur is dry. These could be avoidance behaviors. For more information on this topic, see page 191 in Chapter 5: Troubleshooting.

Dog in the search field, loose leash, food remaining nearby.

The Search Field

Undesirable Behavior: Dog Works Outside the Search Field

Observations	Interpretation	Correction (A) current track (B) future track
Deep nose, focused, only briefly outside the search field		(A) No correction is needed as long as he works carefully.
Moves further and further away from the search field, becomes restless, eventually raises his head	Dog has not yet understood the connection between the location of treats and shoe prints.	(A) Block with the leash and eventually show the treats. Keep practicing.
		(B) Let the dog watch the search field being laid as it increases motivation.
Moves away from the search field against the wind	Not yet enough experience with wind.	
	Possibly interesting smells in the wind or on the ground.	(A) Block with the leash and maybe show the treats. Keep practicing.

Undesirable Behavior: Dog Lifts Head in Search Field

Observations	Interpretation	Correction (A) current track (B) future track
Dog lifts his head	Dog has not yet understood that lifting the head is undesirable.	(A) Praise repeatedly when the dog tracks intensively. When/if the dog lifts his head say, "NO!" while pointing downwards. As soon as the dog has his nose down and is searching, say, "Search!". If necessary, say it again and again.
Looks around	Dog is distracted by people and/or dogs.	(A) Use the "No" and "Search" auditory signals. (B) Place the next search field in an environment with less distraction, increasing the attractiveness of treats.
Looks around	There are only few treats left in the search field.	(A) Finish the exercise as soon as possible after further treats intake or quickly sprinkle more treats without the dog noticing.
After searching for a while, the dog's tail may drop and his body tension decreases and stops		(A) Say "No" while pointing down, and follow up by saying "Search." Finish the exercise as soon as possible. After further treats intake, praise the dog and show pronounced joy.

Smells into the wind	This behavior may be a breed-related track behavior, e.g., hunting dogs search with a high nose.	(A) Say "No" and then "Search" while pointing down. Do this again and again. Be patient. Avoid stressful situations otherwise the dog will increasingly show his breed-related behavior.
		(B) Put a lot of treats on the track first then train the particular behavior in short sessions.
Dog possibly seeks the proximity of the handler. Dog may be exhibiting calming behaviors such as ducking or licking his mouth.		(A) Praise, show treats, provide stress relief.
		(B) Avoid stress by using positive reinforcement training. Another handler can possibly give help to the dog until the dog understands what to do.
Chews		(B) Change treats even though this does not work for all dogs. Some dogs chew even the smallest chunks of treats.
Remains motionless	Dog may exhibit pain during the search.	(B) Veterinarian or physiotherapist may need to examine the dog.
Remains motionless, possibly lifts front paw forward.	Pointing behavior is typical in hunting dogs when they smell game.	(A) Use the "No" and "Search" auditory signals as described above.

Other Undesirable Behaviors

Behavior	Interpretation	Correction (A) current track (B) future track
Jumps frantically back and forth or bounces excitedly.	The arousal level is too high.	(A) Calm the dog down.
	Treats are not attractive enough. Treats are not perceived and the dog walks past them.	(B) Change treats to one that is greatly valued.

In the search field with the nose not close enough to the ground.

Food Intake

Treats on the track is the number one motivator in tracking training. However, it is often also the reason for a dog showing undesirable behavior during track work. Therefore, invest enough time and care in choosing the reward treats. Many training problems can be solved more easily by choosing suitable treats. Even if the dog tracks intensively without treats, you should have the possibility to support him in the learning process by a specific placement of treats.

Even if you have figured out your dog's favorite treats, the dog may want to charge ahead on the track without picking up those treats. Most of the time, the treats are too small to begin with. The dog is motivated by them but gets more and more agitated because the treats are too small or because he can't find them fast enough. If the treats are large enough for the dog to find easily and small enough not to trigger chewing, the dog is much less agitated. He can focus most of his attention on finding the track.

The dog should eat every piece of food.

Visibly Inconspicuous

The treats should hardly stand out from the terrain, so that the dog does not learn to mainly use his eyes when tracking. Cheese pieces are, therefore, somewhat problematic. They should be used only in exceptional cases, for example, when there are no substitute treats of equal value from the dog's point of view. If you use cheese and you notice that your dog is looking for the cheese pieces with his eyes, hide them a bit in the heel section of the shoe print.

Undesirable Behavior: The Dog Does Not Take All the Treats

Further Observation	Location of the Treats Not Taken	Wind Direction
Lifts his head again and again and smells		
Lifts his head again and again, runs back and forth		
Deep nose, quiet, intensive		
Very restless, pulls very strongly		
Lifts his head when eating the treats		
Dog tracks in circles around treats, avoids treats		
Deep nose, quiet, intensive	Treats on the side facing away from the wind are increasingly not picked up.	Strong side wind
Dog tracks only right or left shoe prints	Treats only to the left or right are not picked up.	Often with headwind or tailwind
Treats which do not differ from the ground are not completely picked up	Treats that are hidden in the heel print may not be recognized.	

When Dogs Avoid Treats

Ants, wasps, or beetles are sometimes crawling around on the treats. Some dogs will subsequently avoid the treats if they are stung or bitten by wasps or ants. You should then change either the treats or the terrain.

A few dogs are not motivated by treats when tracking. In that case, choose another type of reward for your dog. Training without treats confirmation is possible, but not described in this book.

Interpretation	Correction (A) current track (B) future track
Dog is too distracted (other dogs, people, etc.), treats not attractive enough.	(A) "No," pointing gesture, possibly "Search." (B) Select environment with less distraction. B) Change treats.
Dog is full or does not like the treats.	(B) Because dog should be hungry for training or change the treats!
Treats are unimportant at the moment.	(B) Increase the attractiveness of treats to have more training opportunities.
Dog is too excited.	(A) Hold dog with leash and show treats. (B) Use larger treats, stronger smelling treats, possibly also change treat types.
Treats may be too large if the dog chews the treats.	(B) Change treats, e.g., use softer treats. In some dogs this behavior cannot be changed.
Dog may have had a negative experience with treats such as ant bite, bee sting, beetle infestation.	(B) Change terrain or change the treats so that the dog forgets the experience. Be patient!
Dog does not notice the treats.	(A) Show treats. (B) Reduce pace width.
Dog smells the next treats too early due to headwinds.	(A) Show the dog any treats and make it clear that he should take-in any. (B) Reduce pace width or increase pace length. Increase the attractiveness of the treats. Put treats to the right and left in shoe prints.
Dog tracks treats strongly with his eyes, not with his nose.	Change the size of the treats.

Other Undesirable Behaviors

Behavior	Wind Direction	Interpretation	Correction (A) current track (B) future track
Dog walks back to not taken treats	Often with tailwind	Search speed is too fast in relation to the reaction time of the dog.	(A) Slow down search speed by pulling on the leash. Possibly prevent dog from following the track against the laying direction. Step on not eaten treats, so they are "gone."
Dog jumps highly excited from one treat to the next		Indication of an inner conflict of the dog: the dog wants to track but also to eat the treats, he needs too much attention to find the treats, thus his arousal increases.	(B) Increase the surface area of the treats or use stronger smelling treats.
Treats do not cause increased motivation for selected training objectives (e.g., article work)		Handler may misjudge how motivating the treats are for the dog. Also treats may be less motivating in comparison with other treats used.	(B) The handler needs to accurately determine the value or attractiveness of the dog treats used. A dog should not be full when training.

The dog is led at an angle to the starting point so he does not rush ahead.

The dog must examine the starting point extensively to pick up the track.

The Starting Point (Scent pad)

Undesirable Behavior	Further Observation	Wind Direction
Dog examines departure rod and then works the track.		
First lifts head.	Works the starting point.	
Repeatedly lifts his head. **Possibly tail significantly lowered.**	Looks around.	
Repeatedly lifts head despite "No."		
Works the starting point only briefly.	Dog picks up track scent immediately but does eat all the treats at the starting point; he may run forward.	Often with headwind
Immediately picks up the scent without examining the starting point.		
Does not eat the treats at the starting point.	But intensively works the starting point.	

Interpretation	Correction (A) current track (B) future track
Curiosity	(A) At first, do not prevent this behavior. (B) If a dog does this frequently and intensively, stop it with a friendly "stop" auditory signal.
Distraction	(A) "No." (B) The next starting point should have fewer distractions.
Lack of motivation	(B) Change treats.
Lack of confidence	(A) Show treats to the dog. Praise the dog when he takes the treats. Help dog with pointing gestures.
"No" has not resulted in a change of behavior perhaps because the dog does not understand "No."	(B) Because a dog should stop a behavior when "No" is heard, the handler needs to condition the "No" auditory signal outside of track.
Dog likes to track but has learned that after the starting point the track always goes straight ahead.	(A) Hold the dog by blocking the leash, possibly show treats at the starting point. (B) To keep the dog from simply following straight out of the track, start him from the side of the starting point. Keep changing sides. (B) At the starting point, possibly use a higher value or tastier treats or bury the treat. (B) Possibly lay two outgoing fields one after the other.
Training at the starting point was insufficient.	(B)Teach the starting point correctly by putting treats at the starting point and approaching the starting point from the side.
Low value or unmotivating treats. Dog tracks enthusiastically.	(B) Change the treats. (B) Pay special attention to whether the behavior at the starting point changes at the next tracks, if unchanged then change treats.

Undesirable Behavior	Further Observation	Wind Direction
Leaves the starting point in the wrong direction.	Dog shows a very hesitant and unsure tracking.	
Does not take up the scent of the track, but works.		
Shows no track behavior, remains standing.	Shows calming signals or panic or avoidance behaviors.	

Interpretation	Correction (A) current track (B) future track
Either the terrain/ environment is too difficult or the track is too challenging.	(A) Help with pointing gestures but stop if necessary. (B) Lay the next starting field more clearly or choose easier terrain. (B) Possibly drop treats in the transition to a straight line.
	(A) Help with pointing gestures but stop if necessary. (B) Design an easier next track.
Dog is overwhelmed and under pressure. He possibly had some negative experiences on the track.	(B) Start again with very easy short tracks, a lot of treats and patience in order to give the dog a quick feeling of success.
Sometimes these behaviors are consequences of very obsessive training.	(B) Rethink and change the way of training. (B) Visit a veterinarian.
Could be signs of a serious disease such as Lyme Disease or anaplasmosis. Such diseases can result in a change of character among other things.	

Search Speed

The dog should track at a steady speed. He can track quickly or slowly; there are no specifications for this. The search speed must be adapted to the track behavior and the reaction time of the dog. Otherwise undesirable behavior will result, e.g., at the corners. If a dog is too fast at a corner, he may overrun the corner and not follow the route of the track consistently.

Undesirable Behaviors with Regard to the Search Speed

Search Speed	Further Observation	Place on Track	Influence of wind
Very fast	Dog may not take all the treats, nose is down.		
Very fast	Dog may not take all the treats, nose is down.		
Very fast	Dog may not take all the treats, nose is down.		Into the headwind
Very fast	Dog may not take all the treats, nose is down.	Only on difficult or heavily overgrown terrain	
Very fast	Dog walks over corner, after 1-2 paces the dog works in a small arc back to the following straight line and continues tracking there.	At the corner	
Make sure you have conditioned this beforehand.	Dog does not track both right and left shoe prints.		Especially with headwind
Alternating	Possibly slight lifting of the nose	After corners and articles	
Alternating	Possibly slight lifting of the nose, takes few or no treats	On a straight line	

Interpretation	Correction (A) current track (B) future track
Treats are getting too much attention from the dog or are not motivating the dog.	(B) Change treats or use larger sized treats or perhaps use stronger smelling treats.
Reaction time is too slow for search speed.	(A) Slow down the search speed by holding the leash.
Next treats are already perceived.	(B) Push treats in the ground, put treats into heel print and use fewer treats.
Treats are getting too much attention from the dog or are not motivating the dog.	(B) Change type of treat or possibly use a stronger smelling variety.
Search speed too fast in relation to the reaction time of the dog.	(A) Reduce search speed.
Due to wind the track can be detected at an early stage.	(A) Show treats (B) Push treats deeper into terrain or bury small cans of treats.
(A) This behavior happens frequently when the dog has the experience that after a corner or an article the track leads always straight on. (B) There is no motivation for the dog to track intensively.	(A) Incorporate more difficult tasks shortly after corner or articles on the track (e.g. corner, break in track, change of direction). (B) Use a second leash with a second handler who helps stop the dog. This second handler walks next to the corner so he can slow down the dog after the corner. (B) Bury small treat cans. After the corner, put treats on the track. (B) Put more treats shortly after the corner. (B) Use highly motivating or high value treats.
Not much motivation to track.	(B) Make the track more motivating with high value treats. Vary the track layout. Bury small treat cans.

Search Speed	Further Observation	Place on Track	Influence of wind
Alternating	Possibly slight lifting of the nose.		With headwind
Alternating	After terrain changes or road crossings.		
Alternating		As soon as the handler can no longer determine the speed through the leash (acute corners, right corners).	
Very slow	Lift head again and again, nose higher when tracking.		
Dog remains standing			
Dog remains standing	Dog looks to handler.		
Dog remains standing	Dog looks around.		
Dog remains standing	Dog smells into the wind.		

Interpretation	Correction (A) current track (B) future track
	(B) Bury treats.
	(B) Instead of laying the track straight, use slight curves so the dog must be more attentive and follow the track route exactly.
	(B) Again and again put treats in footprints.
Difficulty to track the terrain.	(A) Use leash for speed control.
	(B) Practice.
	(A) Pay special attention to search speed, short leash.
	(B) Intervene via voice.
	(B) Make sure you have conditioned this beforehand.
Low motivation	(B) Apply motivational measures such as changing food, providing play breaks.
Pain? Physical condition problems?	(B) Doctor, Fitness training.
1) Dog is insecure. 2) Dog is helped too much. 3) Track is too difficult.	(A) Encourage dog to stop, possibly helping him by using pointing gestures. (A) Encourage dog to stop. (B) Decrease the difficulty of the next training track.
1) Demotivated 2) Track too difficult. 3) Distraction	(A) Change the treats. Say "No." (B) Lower the difficulty of the next training track, possibly use pointing gesture.
1) Distraction by e.g., game 2) Behavior could be breed related stress because track is too difficult.	(A) Use a pointing gesture, say "No." Use a friendly "No." (B) Lower the difficulty of the training track.

Search Speed	Further Observation	Place on Track	Influence of wind
Dog remains standing		On the corner	

Intensive search behavior, loose leash, food to find remains on the track.

On the Straight Line

Leaving the track is the most common undesirable behavior in track work. In order to be able to react appropriately as a dog handler, it is particularly important to observe exactly at which point of the track and under which external conditions this unwanted behavior occurs.

The dog must first learn that he should use his nose to track for the steps on the ground. Only when this is securely anchored in the dog's behavior can other reasons for leaving the track be considered.

Interpretation	Correction (A) current track (B) future track
1) Dog is helped too much.	(A) Encourage the dog, the handler should stop.
2) There was too much corrective action during the last training tracks.	(A) Encourage dog, handler should stop, eventually using a pointing gesture.
3) Dog is insecure.	(B) Lower difficulty, put more treats also right behind a corner, corner with larger radius.

This is what it should look like, deep nose, quiet confident tracking, following the track exactly.

Undesirable behavior: Dog Searches with Nose to the Right and Left of the Pace Sequence

He does not leave the track with his body (small dog's body is possibly slightly beside the track).

Further Observation	Wind Influence	Interpretation	Correction (A) current track (B) future track
Dog tracks constantly on one side (right or left) next to the steps, intensive track behavior	Strong crosswind, tracks on side away from wind.	Track scent is blown away by wind.	(B) Put more treats on the track in crosswinds. The treats always lead the dog to the track. Practice.
Dog constantly tracks on one side (right or left) next to the steps, occasionally lifts his nose a bit.	Strong crosswind, tracks on wind facing side.	Distraction by odor from wind direction.	(A) Possibly use "No" in case of constant lateral deviation from the track. Use pointing gesture.
Dog tracks sometimes to the right, sometimes to the left of steps oscillating	Strong gusty crosswind.		(B) Practice and put more treats on the track.
Dog tracks sometimes right or left of steps oscillating, tracks in area around track, tail indicates high effort (e.g. strongly lowered)		Too difficult track design for the difficulty of the terrain.	(B) Make difficulty easier through step design, if necessary.
Dog briefly tracks sideways, e.g., mouse hole, rabbit droppings		Dog has not yet understood that handler does not want this behavior.	(A) Use "No" and then "Search."
On straight lines diagonal to terrain structures, e.g., seed furrows.		Harder to track for dog.	(A) Praise when the dog is following the track exactly. (B) Increased practice, preferably in the middle part of the track, so that the dog can show ideal track behavior at the beginning and end of the track. Put more treats on the track.

Undesirable Behavior: Dog Leaves the Track with His Whole Body

Further Observation	Wind Direction	Interpretation	Correction (A) current track (B) future track
Dog tracks in area around track without visibly picking up the track.		Track behavior not properly conditioned, possibly due to constant mild or severe overwhelming.	(A) Return to the starting point, new start. (B)Recondition the dog's track behavior through easy tracks with lots of treats.
Dog tracks in area around track without visibly picking up the scent.		Due to weather conditions (e.g., rain, frost, etc.) or not clearly laid steps, there is hardly any difference in scent between the track and the surrounding terrain for the dog to perceive. He can only guess an approximate area, where smell traces are still present. Within this area, he oscillates back and forth.	(A) Only allow very experienced dog to continue tracking, normally break off track, if possible at the next article, make break-off positive for dog.
Dog tracks only at a small lateral distance from paces, continues to track parallel to the track	Strong crosswind	Scent displacement due to wind.	(B) Put more food on the track so the dog learns to stay on the track. Be patient as changing behaviors may take a long time.
Dog circles in different places and then resumes tracking.		Track difficult.	(A) Shorten the leash and limit the dog's radius of action. (A) Possibly train a problem solving behavior such as teaching the dog to stop and track only with the nose off the track. (A) Praise the dog as soon as he picks up the track again. (B) Determine the exact difficulty the dog is having and then practice this difficulty.
Dog purposefully walks towards something (tuft of grass, food of humans left next to the track, etc.)		Motivation of the dog to track the track is lower than an interesting object outside the track.	(A) Use "No" and "Search."

173

Undesirable Behavior: Dog Lifts Nose or Head

Further Observation	Place on Track	Wind Direction
High nose, turns nose in wind		
Nose significantly higher	In easy to find track sections	
Nose significantly higher		Into the headwind
Nose significantly higher	After a longer track	
Nose significantly higher		
Dog lifts head and looks around		
Dog just stands there, no track effort		

Interpretation	Correction (A) current track (B) future track
Distraction, breed-related behavior may be the cause of problems.	(A) Use "No" and "Search."
Dog is unfocused because the track is easy to find, nothing new anymore, boring. Even easy tracks must be tracked with a deep nose.	(B) Make easier track sections more difficult by including surprising direction changes.
	(B) Put food in the heel steps. Use small cans.
Tired	(B) Do more fitness training with the dog. Use more food towards the end of the track. Consider pushing food deeper in the ground/terrain.
Dog tracks with eyes, track was too often very clearly visible, treats visible.	(B) Food must not stand out from the terrain in terms of color. Do not train visible tracks.
Distraction by people, animals, etc., on and off the track.	(A) "No," "Search" or show track (B) If very frequent head lifting on a training track, lay the next training track with lower external distraction. Change the treats.
1) Demotivated, exhausted 2) Fear of mistakes/punishment 3) Dog gives up, not persistent in solving problems 4) Internal conflict 5) Sick	(A) Break off track with positive experience (B) Reduce difficulty significantly, short tracks or only squares (B) Reconsider training method (A) Encourage the dog to continue tracking, possibly break off the track with a positive experience. (B) Reduce difficulty significantly, slowly increase fitness condition (A) Encourage dog to track, do not create further stress (B) Vet visit

Undesirable Behavior: Dog Does Not Track Every Pace

Further Observations	Wind Direction	Interpretation	Correction (A) current track (B) future track
Dog tracks only one side in case of right-left offset of paces, eventually changes sides.		Treats degraded too quickly.	(B) Use more treats right and left to control the track behavior.
		Pace width increased too quickly.	(B) Reduce pace width again so that dog tracks every step. Put more treats into individual paces. Alternatively, increase pace length.
		In some training tracks not all treats are picked up.	(B) Design training track so that all treats are picked up.
	Headwind	Next but one pace is already perceived.	(B) Reduce pace width. Step treats into soil. Bury small treat cans.
Dog constantly tracks only one side in case of right-left offset of the paces.	Crosswind	Dog perceives the right and left prints due to the crosswind, even if the dog does not examine the step directly; there is too little incentive (treats) to examine right and left steps directly. The dog has not yet learned to track exactly the track.	(B) Reinforce treats in paces right and left, distributing them irregularly.

Ideally, the dog should track with a deep nose. There are also dogs that generally track with a slightly lifted nose. It is assumed that for them the smell of the track is most intensive there. These dogs do not show any track behavior with a deep nose at any point of the track, not even at especially challenging sections. This behavior is probably hard to extinguish, but very rare. Almost always a dog's lifted nose when tracking is the result of not optimal training.

Even with high vegetation, the nose should always be close to the ground.

The Corners

The handler must know exactly the position of the corner. Only then can he analyze his dog's behavior and make appropriate corrections. The treats should not be directly in the area of the corner, so that the dog's full attention is focused on tracking the corner.

In general, if a dog has difficulty with a corner, analyze the situation. Pace length, pace width, wind direction, location in the terrain, type of terrain, etc.

If your dog shows strong signs of insecurity, support him by pointing, blocking the leash, encouraging and providing more treats on the next track, among other things. For the next training track, decrease the difficulty of the corners slightly so that your dog can track the track easily or more easily. Focus on optimal track behavior at corners. The dog should learn calm, confident, and exact tracking of corners from the beginning.

Slightly lifted nose while tracking.

Undesirable behavior: Dog does not follow change of direction at the corner right away

Dog continues to track straight across the corner, stops shortly after the corner, tracks right and left (possibly circles), after some time finds the next straight line and continues to track.

Further Observation	Wind Direction	Interpretation	Correction (A) current track (B) future track
Dog lifts his head and runs back and forth.	For all wind directions	Corner is too difficult. Dog shows stress-related behavior which is possibly typical for the breed.	(A) Block the leash. Restrict action radius and use pointing gestures and verbal support. (B) Decrease difficulty of corner (larger radius of corner, smaller pace length, smaller pace width).
Intensive track behavior	For all wind directions	Corner is too difficult, possibly because the search speed is too high.	(A) Block leash. Restrict action radius and possibly use pointing gestures or verbal support. Reduce search speed. (B) Decrease difficulty of corner (larger radius of corner, smaller pace length, smaller pace width).
	Mainly with tailwind	Corner is too difficult. Tail wind blows odor after corner straight ahead first.	(A) Block leash. Restrict action radius. Possibly use pointing gestures or verbal support, practice. (B) Decrease difficulty of corner (larger radius of the corner, smaller pace length, smaller pace width). Train tailwind.
	Mainly with crosswind, e.g., corner leads to the left and the wind comes from the right.	Corner is too difficult. Crosswind blows the track scent away sideways.	(A) Block leash. Restrict action radius. Possibly use pointing gestures or verbal support. Practice. (B) Decrease difficulty of corner (larger radius of the corner, smaller pace length, smaller pace width). Specifically train crosswinds. Place treats shortly after the corner and in almost every step.

Further Observation	Wind Direction	Interpretation	Correction (A) current track (B) future track
		Search speed is too fast in relation to the reaction time of the dog.	(A) Reduce search speed by keeping the leash taut. (B) Condition the auditory signal "Slow." Put more treats on the track.
The dog lifts his nose or head just before a corner.		Inattention is due to other impressions and stimuli.	(A) Use the auditory signals "No," "Search." Keep the leash taut.

Undesirable Behavior: Dog Continues to Track Straight ahead Despite Change of Direction of the Track (Corner)

Further Observation	Wind Direction	Interpretation	Correction (A) current track (B) future track
Deep nose, looks like intense tracking		1) Handler did not know where the exact corner was during training, and made no or inappropriate corrections. 2) Dog did not find the track and did not indicate this out of fear of punishment.	(A) Have exact knowledge of the track. (B) At the next track lay a corner in such a way that the dog can track the corner without any problems. Rethink the training style. There should be no coercion on the trail.
Dog shows signs of uncertainty after the corner (e.g., hesitation, tail lowers, etc.), turns to the right or left, continues tracking in a circle and turns onto the next straight when he has found it.	Tailwind, sometimes crosswind	1) Change of direction is too fast (radius is too small) for the dog's level of training. 2) This is the problem-solving strategy of the dog, which he has become accustomed to. He should stop and initially work the track only with the nose.	(A) Block the leash, possibly help the dog. (B) Design corners with larger radius and smaller pace length. Practice appropriate problem-solving behaviors.

Other Undesirable Behaviors

Further Observation	Wind Direction	Interpretation	Correction (A) current track (B) future track
Dog does not track to the top of the corner but changes to the next straight line prematurely.	Headwind	Dog already smells the course of the next straight line.	(A) Block with leash. Make a disapproving noise. Possibly show track. (B) Possibly put treats until just before the corner, and then again relatively far behind the corner.
Dog accelerates after the corner.		Dog has the common experience that after a corner the track continues straight ahead.	(A) Block the leash. Use the auditory signal "Slow" (only when this auditory signal is already conditioned). (B) Vary the design of the tracks (e.g., serpentine lines): shortly after a corner another corner, or shortly after corner bury small treat cans, etc.
Dog hesitates briefly after a corner.		He has not yet become accustomed to confident track behavior at the corner. Corners are too challenging.	(A) Encourage dog with voice. (B) Lower the difficulty of the corners until the dog repeatedly shows confident track behavior without hesitation at the corners. Place treats shortly after corner.
He comes back after the corner.		Dog shows insecure track behavior.	(A) Block dog by body position. Walk close behind the dog. Possibly use a pointing gesture in track direction. (B) Make the difficulty of the corners easier until the dog repeatedly shows confident track behavior without hesitation at the corners. Use increased treats after the corner.

Further Observation	Wind Direction	Interpretation	Correction (A) current track (B) future track
The dog hesitates after a corner and does not track the following straight line immediately, if the following straight line is oblique to terrain structures.		Practiced too little in training.	(A) Encourage dog. (B) Lay more corners with subsequent straight line obliquely to terrain structures. Possibly decrease difficulty of the paces. Practice.
He hesitates after a corner and does not look for the following straight line immediately. The corner is very close to a terrain change or road crossing.		Practiced too little in training.	(A) Encourage dog. (B) Practice this situation more often. Possibly decrease the difficulty of the paces.

Indicate Articles

The dog should indicate articles convincingly. What convincing means is not exactly described in the trial regulations. Therefore, only undesirable behaviors that are criticized as such in the majority of cases are described as undesirable behaviors in this chapter. Again, it is important to observe your dog and the circumstances closely. What do you see? What is, among other things, the wind direction, the position of the article or the material of the article? Only then analyze his behavior.

It is easier to teach the dog the correct indicating behavior with the appropriate beginning than to correct faulty indicating later.

Always closely watch your dog's reaction to corrections. Show your dog clearly what you expect from him. Do not let him stand by the article in uncertainty. Avoid coercive measures. They lead to avoidance behavior or unmotivated indicating.

Letting others know the dog has indicated the article.

Undesirable Behavior: Dog Does Not Indicate Article

Further Observation	Interpretation	Correction (A) current track (B) future track
Dog does not show any reaction to the article.	Dog has not yet sufficiently learned to indicate. He does not yet know for sure what is expected of him. Aids were reduced too fast.	(B) Teach the dog to indicate correctly and patiently from the beginning, possibly also outside the track.
	1) Material of the article is unknown.	(A) Block leash and show article. (B) Train different materials.
	2) It is an article from a stranger.	(A) Block leash and show article. (B) Train stranger's articles.
	3) Location of the article is outside the scent area.	(A) Block leash and show article. B) Train very different positions.
	4) The dog's attention is too much focused on the track.	(A) Block leash and show article. (B) Do indicating training initially mainly on easy tracks
Dog shows a slight reaction (e.g., hesitation), but then continues to track without indicating.	1) Material of the article is unknown.	(A) Block leash and show article. (B) Train very different materials.
	2) It is an article from a stranger.	A) Block leash and show article. (B) Train stranger's articles.
	3) Dog prefers to track.	
	4) Dog has not yet understood indicating.	(A) Block leash and show article. Give a special reward for indicating (e.g., delicious treats).
	5) The article is not an article for the dog, reason unknown.	(A) Teach indicating again from the beginning with all aids. (B) Patience. Practice. Identify reasons from the dog's perspective.
	Dog associates unpleasant experiences with incorrect indication and therefore shows avoidance behaviors.	(A) Ask the dog in a friendly way to indicate. Do not force. Give special treats.
	The dog thinks that he should indicate only an article which is rewarded with treats.	(A) Train without and with treats. Have patience and give lots of praise.

Other Undesirable Behaviors

Undesirable Behavior	Further Observation	Wind Problems
Dog shows restless behavior at the article (especially when standing).		
Dog lies/stands/sits oblique to the track.		Strong cross wind
Dog shows strong oblique indicating.	Mostly connected with the dog turning around to the handler	
Dog indicates too slowly.	First lowering the front torso, then lowering the rear torso section	
		Especially in case of wet, "dirty" terrain
Dog is too far away from the article.		Especially in the headwind
	For indicating type "Sit"	

Interpretation	Correction (A) current track (B) future track
1) Dog handler shows uncoordinated behavior. 2) It is the wrong type of indicating for the type of dog.	1) (A) Practice the following movements: Reward quickly, hold treats in hand already during the straight line, no jerky movements of the handler. Possibly practice "Stand" reliably beforehand. 1) (B) Possibly change indicating type.
Due to the wind, the dog is not exactly on the track and then turns his body when indicating the article.	(A) Possibly go back to general teaching of a correct indicating position (off the track), so that the dog corrects himself. Change the side on which you approach the dog when indicating. Possibly step over the dog, one foot to the right, one foot to the left of the dog (only if the dog then does not show avoidance behavior).
Handler always goes to the same side of the dog when the dog indicates.	(A) Change the side on which the handler approaches the dog when indicating. (B) Teach the dog to fixate on the article constantly and not to turn to the handler. Disadvantage: dog has no more relaxation time and tenses up more easily.
Typical lying down for the individual dog.	(B) Check off-track how the dog lies down when given the "Down" signal. Train off-track how to lie down quickly (without coercion).
It is unpleasant for dog.	(B) Check how the dog lies down when hearing the auditory signal "Down" on "dirty" ground. Train fast lying down off the track (without coercion). Possibly change indicating type to "Stand" or "Sit."
Dog has not yet understood the correct position in relation to the article. He smells the article prematurely.	(A) Move the dog to the correct distance from the article. Do not change the position of the article. (B) Outside the track condition "point," where the dog independently tracks the article and indicates it.
Dog pulls front legs to hind legs when sitting and not the other way around.	(B) Change indicating type or accept distance.

Undesirable Behavior	Further Observation	Wind Problems
Dog indicates non-existent articles or stones, corn stubble, plastic pieces, feathers, etc.		
Article is under the chest, under the torso or behind the dog.		Strong tailwind
Dog picks up the article and/or plays around with it.		
Dog changes the position of the article.		
Dog independently resumes working the track.		
Dog shakes himself (wet fur or avoidance behavior).		
Dog eats grass.	Mostly occurs during trials	
Dog picks up an article but does not hand it over (disqualification).		
Dog lays down unusually slowly or spins around several times, or exhibits other unusual behaviors.	When lying down	
Dog walks around the article and continues to track.		

Interpretation	Correction (A) current track (B) future track
1) There might be incorrect conditioning. 2) It could be a stress response. 3) It could be a coercive reaction.	(A) Send the dog on without conditioned auditory signals, e.g., with an encouraging "Come on now." (B) Desensitize on training tracks. Consciously lead the track over things lying in the terrain. Do not touch them; otherwise they will take on the human scent. (B) Identify and desensitize stress factors. (B) Reconsider training method.
Dog has a too high search speed in relation to the reaction time of the dog.	(A) Reduce search speed in tailwind by holding the leash.
Stress symptom leads to playing with article; it might be genetic.	(A) "No" (A) "No" (A) Block leash. Return dog to indicating position (no coercion). Reward indicating position. Vary how long the dog has to indicate (shorter and longer). Possibly teach the dog to look at the handler first and to continue tracking only after "search" (e.g., stand in front of the dog and feed him).
Reasons might be weather (wet!) or avoidance behavior due to stress.	(A) Make no correction or only friendly, disapproving noise.
Reason might be avoidance behavior due to stress.	(A) "No" (B) Identify and desensitize stressors or eliminate these factors. (B) Practice outside the track
Reason might be musculoskeletal disease such as osteoarthritis or genital issues.	(B) See a veterinarian.
Dog experienced something unpleasant associated with the articles such as ant bites while eating treats. Dog shows avoidance behavior.	(A) Identify and avoid negative associations. Lead dog to article and reward with high-value.

The Cross Track

The handler must know exactly where and how the cross track was laid, what the wind direction is when tracking, what design the corner between the cross track and the track is, and what the influencing weather conditions are (frost, rain, etc.). Only then can he judge what his dog has already learned and what he still needs to train. Cross track training should be repeated over and over again. Regularly have helpers lay cross tracks for you.

Undesirable Behaviors at Cross Tracks

Undesirable Behavior	Interpretation
Dog changes to the cross track without hesitation.	1) Dog has not yet understood what to look for or what the difference is between the two tracks.
	2) Wind comes from the direction of the cross track.
	3) Cross track is much more clearly perceptible than the original track.
Dog changes to the cross track and continues to track restlessly on it.	Dog notices that the smell has changed but cannot solve this problem.
Dog enters the cross track up to max. 1 m/3 feet, then turns around, and continues to follow the original track.	1) Dog has understood what to do but still takes too long to decide.
	2) Dog has not yet learned an ideal problem solving behavior.
Dog lifts his head at the intersection and sniffs the wind.	Dog is insecure.
Dog circles at the cross track intersection.	Dog is insecure.
Dog shows no reaction at all to cross track.	Dog does not perceive cross track, thus there is no training effect.

The dog has found the cross track and continues to track confidently.

Correction
(A) current track
(B) future track

1) (A) Block the dog with a leash. Let the dog track as long as he is tracking. Praise as soon as he picks up the original track.

2) (B) Practice all cross track possibilities.

3) (A) Help with pointing gestures. Praise as soon as he picks up the original track.

3) (B) Practice first in the headwind. Increase difficulty slowly.

(A) Block with leash. Possibly help if the dog stops feeling uncertain. Otherwise let the dog continue tracking until he picks up the original track again. Then praise him.

1) (A) Block with leash. Let the dog track as long as he needs to. Praise as soon as he picks up the original track.

2) (B) Practice problem solving behavior (dog stops as long as he investigates the crossing).

(A) Handler should help the dog. He should not cause additional stress by reprimanding the dog when the dog gets back on the track. Praise your dog.

(A) Handler should help the dog. He should not cause additional stress by reprimanding the dog, when the dog gets back on the track, praise your dog.

(B) Lay the next cross track more intensively.

Road Crossings

It is desirable that the dog does not lift his nose in the area of crossing the path and simply walks over it. He should have his nose close to the ground. He should make an effort to detect any scent traces that may be present in the area of the path as well, and resume the track after the path with his nose still low.

Crossing a road keeping his nose down on the track.

Undesirable Behaviors at Road Crossings

Undesirable Behavior	Interpretation	Correction (A) current track (B) future track
Dog does not change to the other side of the path, but always tracks for the scent only in front of the path.	Dog has no experience with road crossings.	(B) Line each step with treats in front of the path and in the direct area of the path.
Dog lifts his head and stops tracking, especially if the path is made of concrete or asphalt.	Dog has no experience yet that the track continues after the path.	(A) Show dog the further track. (B) Line each pace in the area of the path with treats.
Dog lifts his head and walks to the other side of the path without tracking.	Dog knows that the track continues on the other side, but has no incentive to continue tracking in the area of the road crossing.	(B) Line each pace in the area of the path with treats.
Dog leaves the track and may mark.	Dog gets distracted by the smells along the way (e.g., marking smells from other dogs).	(A) Use auditory signals "No," "Search."

Avoidance Behaviors

Avoidance behaviors, such as eating grass, are stress and conflict related observed over and over again during trials.

According to Nikolaus Tinbergen, an avoidance behavior is a "... behavior as an expression of a conflict between two instincts. Therefore, the continuation of the previously observable instinctual behavior is temporarily not possible and instead a behavior is exhibited that originates from a completely different functional circle of the behavioral repertoire."

Accordingly, an avoidance behavior does not match the action already shown. It does not fit into any stimulus-action context. It gives the dog time and a short escape from the conflict.

Avoidance behaviors during tracking work can be:

- Eating during the track
- Shaking at the article even in dry weather
- Asking the handler to play
- Standing still while tracking and scratching

Scratching is a possible avoidance behavior.

Identifying Reasons

However, the described actions are always ambiguous. In the case of shaking, the reason could also be a wet coat, and scratching a symptom of illness. It is sometimes difficult to judge whether a behavior is avoidance behavior or not.

If it is a real avoidance behavior, it is usually not very useful to wean the dog off this action. He will express his inner conflict by another action, which may be much more disturbing. It makes more sense to find out what kind of conflict your dog is experiencing. Then you can avoid it. The most promising training is one that helps the dog approach a conflict with confidence and solve problems without much stress.

If the dog predominantly shows avoidance behaviors during trials, the handler should possibly work on his own stress related issues. Maybe the dog reacts stressed in the trial situation only because his handler is stressed.

Mutual trust and a good relationship are the basis of successful tracking training.

6. Tracking Trials

Together in a Trial Situation

Trial Regulations

Many handlers, in addition to training with their dog, want to compete against other teams. In tracking, there are trials for tracking dogs with different levels. Those are described in the international trial regulations. You can find the most current test regulations at vdh.de or fci.be. (This website refers to Germany's kennel club, similar to the American Kennel Club- AKC). During a trial, the performance of the dog and the handler is evaluated. 100 points are the highest achievable outcome. Requirement for all trials is a passed companion test. For some singular tracking trials there are further requirements. There is also a minimum age for the dog.

Requirements

The following remarks refer to the IGP requirements as of 2019. The track behavior is the same for all levels. "The dog should pick up the scent with a deep nose and follow the course in a motivated manner, with a deep nose, high track intensity, persistently and steadily. Search speed is not a criterion if the dog works intensively and convincingly." These criteria leave some room for interpretation. It is not stated which behavior is directly required.

Trial situation, pure tension for the handler, hopefully not for the dog.

Requirement	Observable Behavior
Deep	Nose as close to the ground as possible, examines every shoe print
Motivated	Nonspecific, overall body posture
High track intensity	Nonspecific, tense body posture
Continuous	No disruption in tracking
Consistent	Consistent search speed over the course of the entire track, in the case of very different terrain with possibly changing level of difficulty, a change of speed is permissible
Intensive	Nonspecific, see high track intensity
Convincing	Nonspecific

As you can see, the description of the track behavior in the IGP is quite vague which means that there are many different evaluation criteria. What is considered intensive tracking for a beagle, looks possibly quite different for a German Shepherd. For some dogs, intensive tracking shows by lowering of the tail; others show this by a high tail. For you as the dog handler it is important that you can interpret your dog's body language.

Trails Run by Dog Clubs

Trials are run by different dog clubs. For all, the international test regulation of the FCI applies. Depending on the dog club, there are different requirements and interpretations of the test rules. If possible, consult an experienced dog handler regarding what is common practice at the dog club where you'd like to compete. The further you get, possibly to the World Championships, the more you will realize that evaluations of transregional trials differ from evaluations of local trials. The judges are more rigorous and penalize even the smallest mistakes with deducting points.

After the tracking work: Now the evaluation follows.

Trial Preparation

A trial situation has its own rules and requirements for both the dog and the handler. It is important to prepare for this. If you are sure you don't want to compete, just skip this chapter. Or you may read it and might afterwards be fascinated by the challenge and want to experience it for yourself: Working with your dog under trial conditions. And these conditions have it all.

Talking spectators, many with barking dogs, can be a distraction.

The difference of a test situation to training:

- The handler is usually very nervous (even if he himself does not always perceive this).
- The dog may be either unsettled or very nervous because of this.
- The dog handler must behave according to the requirements of the trial regulations. It is prescribed exactly what he may or may not do.
- The handler must be 10 meters /32 feet behind the dog.
- Spectators, cars, and dogs linger at the edge of the site.
- In the field there is the judge and possibly the track layer.
- There are no treats on the track.
- The scent pad marker is strange to the dog.
- The terrain is unknown.
- Praise is allowed only at a few points of the track work.
- The articles are laid out by the track layer depending on the level of the trial and smell like the track layer.
- The design and shape of the track is unknown to the handler. This is usually a very unsettling feeling for the handler
- The dog may be in the car for a few hours before it is his turn.
- At large national trials, dogs and handlers stay overnight in a hotel or rented house before and during the trial days.

Train together with your dog each of these points, as far as possible.

Practice Beforehand

Specifically, this means:

- Walk 10 meters / 32 feet behind the dog during training.

- The handler must know and practice the correct way to lead the dog in accordance with the trial regulations. It is harder than you think. It is helpful to have a dog handler who is experienced in trials observe you.

- The dog should also correctly track for longer passages without treats. However, the treats should never be completely removed during training. Possibly a track without treats can be tracked before the first trial track (but not directly before), so that the handler can assess the behavior of his dog under this condition.

- Train the trial situation with the help of other dog handlers or helpers: especially spectators, performance judges and track layers, cars at the edge of the track area, barking dogs, etc. This is very important especially for handlers who train mainly alone.

- If you want to compete at a level with a stranger`s track (track is laid by a track layer, not by you), have a track laid by an experienced person. This person should have recent competing experience. The way of laying tracks has changed a lot in the last few years. The track layer must be able to tell you at all times during training where exactly the track and the articles are located.

- In training, praise on individual straight lines only occasionally.

- Develop a routine that gets your dog in the mood for track work.

- Your dog should be able to spend a few hours relaxed in the car and after a preparation phase be able to track in a focused manner.

- Practice reporting in with the judge at the beginning of the trial.

- Use a wide variety of strangers' articles. Even brand new ones!

Reporting in before the trail begins.

Dog leaves the starting point, handler remains standing.

Two Frequently Asked Questions

When Is an Appropriate Time to Compete?

The dog should be able to reliably perform according to the trial requirements. Since both the handler and the dog are under stress during a trial, the dog often shows different behavior during the trial than during training. The stress unsettles many dogs and they no longer show their usual training performance. On the other hand, there are dogs that track more motivated in a trial than in training. They show better track performance than in training. You will find out which type your dog is at your first trial.

Before a trial, slowly reduce the treats, but never completely. Do not place any treats at all on some straight lines, and place treats again sporadically on the following straight lines. There are no treats on the trial track. Your dog should already know this situation in part and still track intensively.

Before a trial, you should only track easier tracks in training, so that your dog can show his correct track behavior. Only after a trial can new requirements and difficulties be incorporated into the training tracks.

When Should the Dog Track His Last Training Track Before the Trial?

It depends on the dog. It is best to keep the usual interval between tracking training tracks. Also keep the usual daily routine with feeding times. If your dog does not get treats before training on a training day, he will not get any before tracking on a trial day. If he gets his normal treats during the day on training days, he should also get them on trial days.

Behavior of the Dog Handler

Not only the dog but also the handler is evaluated during a trial track. The behavior of both the dog and the handler is strongly regulated during a trial. Mistakes usually result in points being deducted. Therefore, it is imperative that you know what correct behavior looks like during a trial. You must practice it beforehand.

Handler waits until the end of the leash is reached.

Below you will find both a description in keywords of the required behavior of the dog handler according to the IGP as well as additions that have proven themselves in practice.

What a Dog Handler Can Expect

- Give the dog the opportunity to move, urinate, defecate, and drink.

- The handler reports to the judge with his dog prepared for the track work (metal link collar, possibly harness on, 10 meters / 32 foot leash unrolled). The dog is in the basic position next to him. The dog may also be brought to the report on a short leash, but must then be made ready to track. Attention: Do not use a sharp auditory signal (coercion is prohibited).

- Handler gives his name and the name of his dog, whether the dog indicates or picks up the articles and the trial level.

Reporting in correctly.

- A short leash must be carried.

- The handler walks as close as possible to his dog to the scent pad marker, giving an auditory signal "Search." His dog begins to track.

- The handler remains standing until he has the end of the 10 meters / 32 foot leash in his hand. Only then may he follow his dog.

- Any assistance by the handler (pointing gestures, body movements, stepping on the leash, etc.) is not allowed.

- The handler must also maintain the 10 meters / 32 foot distance to the dog in the area of a corner. He may leave the track and walk an arc. However, this must only be done when his dog is consistently working the following straight line.

- If the dog indicates an article, the handler drops the leash and walks to his dog. Whether he goes to the dog's right side or left side is not specified.

- He takes the article in his hand, holds it up, puts it in a jacket/shorts pocket, looks at the judge and waits for a sign from the judge that he can continue the track work. He may praise or pet the dog before or after showing the article. The dog must not leave his position.

- He stands next to his dog, takes the leash in his hand, waits a bit and gives the auditory signal "Search."

- The handler remains standing until the dog is 10 meters / 32 feet away from him again which means until he holds the end of the leash in his hand.

- The handler must always follow his dog, even if the dog leaves the track. If he nevertheless holds him back, he will be admonished by the judge to follow his dog. He should follow the judge's instructions.

- When the dog has indicated the last article and the handler has checked with the judge that the end of the track has been reached, the handler makes it clear to his dog that the tracking work is finished. He praises him. Then he goes with his dog to the judge. He hands over the found articles while his dog sits next to him in the basic position. He declares the tracking work finished.

- He takes the evaluation of the performance judge.

- Only then may he play with his dog or feed him. He is not allowed to carry the treats or toy on the track beforehand.

- After the tracking work, the dog must have the opportunity to move, urinate, defecate, and drink.

- Do some stretching exercises.

And off we go: The dog handler remains standing at first...

... and follows her dog at the end of the 32 foot leash.

Further Possible Situations

In addition to this general behavior of the dog handler during trial, there are many situations in which a dog handler should have informed himself about the correct behavior beforehand. It is useful to practice this behavior. Here is a small overview of possible situations and the correct behavior of the dog handler.

Situation	Correct Behavior
Behavior when game appear.	"Down." Auditory signal allowed, continue tracking after some time.
Dog is tangled in the leash.	Obtain permission from judge, release dog, auditory signal possible but do not grab leash near the dog but at the end of leash.
Dog comes back to the handler on the track.	Stand still, in no case shorten the leash.
Dog does not go off at the starting point.	Use a second auditory signal.

Out on the track: The dog, handler, judge and track layer.

If in doubt, help your dog on the track. Even if you then possibly do not pass the trial, it is usually better for the dog to receive help instead of feeling unsettled in the trial situation by the fact that the handler no longer does or says anything in problem situations. Most of the time the judge tolerates it if the handler gives his dog auditory signals and deducts a few points for unauthorized assistance. There are countless opportunities to behave incorrectly unintentionally, and sometimes without even realizing it. Often the following behaviors lead to points being deducted:

Mistakes on the Part of the Dog Handler:

- Waiting too short at the restart after indicating the article.

- Not waiting at the restart for the performance judge's signal when starting again after the article has been picked up.

- Dog indicates and the handler walks forward on the leash lying on the ground.

- Praising the dog at the corner.

- Blocking the dog by the body posture when indicating.

- Any kind of pointing gestures on the track or at the article.

- Handler does not follow the dog (e.g., when following the cross track), but blocks the leash. This is followed by an admonition from the judge to follow the dog. If the handler does not follow this instruction, the tracking work is terminated.

- Shortening the leash, i.e., the handler no longer holds the leash at the end, but further forward. He often does that without noticing. It is also often considered a shortening of the leash if the entire length of the leash touches the ground, even if the handler has the end of the leash in his hand.

- Jerking of the leash by the dog handler.

- Repeated auditory signal "Search," when the dog is no longer tracking; the auditory signal is allowed at the start and after each indicating.

Evaluation of the Dog's Tracking by the Judge

Evaluating the track is done by the judge after the track has been completed. He describes how the dog mastered the individual parts of the track (straight lines, corners, article work, etc.), what behavior he showed and what mistakes he made. He also evaluates the behavior of the handler. Was it according to the rules or not? The maximum score is 100 points. For different mistakes on the track there is a different point deduction. At the end of the evaluation, the performance judge states the number of points achieved. The exact distribution of points is usually not apparent from what has been said. Depending on the dog association, individual requirements of the trial regulations are interpreted differently. Do not be discouraged if the judge sees and evaluates some things differently than you do. The dog handler should follow the evaluation closely and possibly draw conclusions for the further training.

Intensive track in front of a corner...   *..and here it goes right into the next leg.*

Felix and the Corners

Felix is trained to take the corner exactly even in a strong headwind and not to shorten it. During a trial, he works his way up to the corner in the headwind and checks again and again with his nose whether the corner is already coming up (in the headwind, he smells it early). Only when he is exactly at the corner, he turns. The judge deducts points from his score for not tracking the corner purposefully. But the handler is proud of his dog, who has worked out the corner exactly as he taught him.

For more details on the distribution of points on a track and other evaluation criteria, please refer to the currently valid trial regulations.

And despite all the stress of the trial: experience yourself and your dog as a team and be fascinated by your dog's skills.

About the Author

Ute C. Fallscheer is an active dog sports woman and trainer in the field of tracking work. She has successfully handled Border Terriers for more than 15 years and is a multiple Bavarian IPO FH champion (blv) and German champion (KfT). She has also qualified countless times for the VDH and dhv championships and has repeatedly placed very well. She was also a substitute starter for Germany at the IPO FH World Championship in Jessen.

Ute C. Fallscheer passes on her training and trial experience in tracking seminars for dogs of all breeds. Her seminars on "Focus: Dog Handler," which focus on how to train the dog handler, have also met with a positive response. She is the author of the book "Der Weg zum guten Hundefuehrer" ("The Path to Being a Good Dog Handler"). Her website is: fallscheer-aalen.de

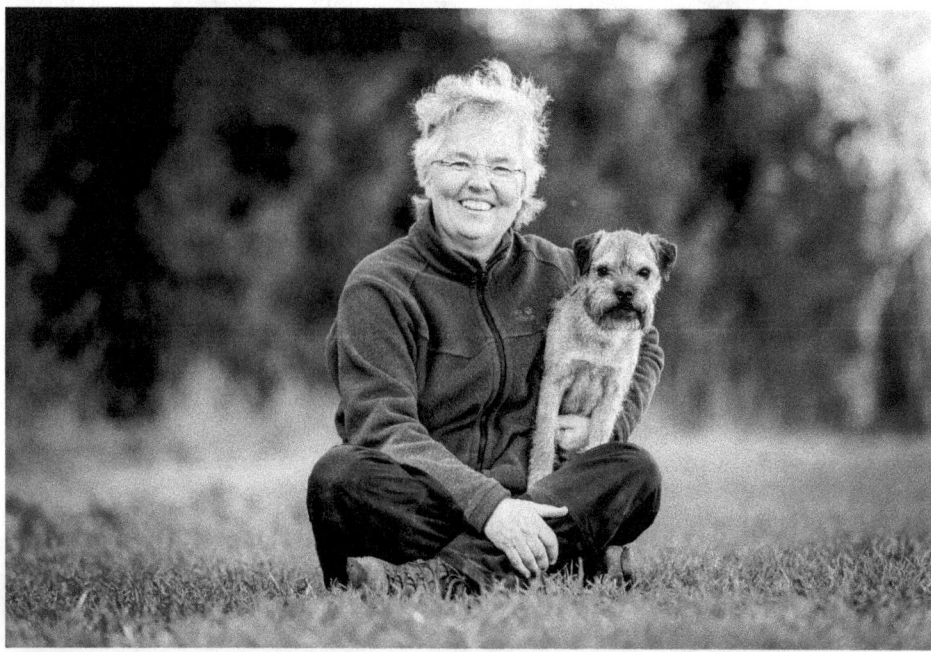

Acknowledgments

This book would not have been possible without the experiences in tracking training with many dog handlers and their dogs. Thanks to all of you.

I would especially like to thank my husband Herbert and our daughter Lea, who have always encouraged and actively supported me.

Britta Elser, Heike and Uwe Ritthammer and Gütha Schwalbach have tirelessly read through my manuscript drafts and provided valuable suggestions. Thank you for your constructive feedback.

And not forgetting the dog handlers and their dogs, who took a lot of time for the photo shoot and braved the cold weather. Thank you Andrea, Britta, Daniel, Gloria, Jennifer, Lucia, Sebastian, Sonja, Steffi, Uschi and Uwe, as well as Albert Kortmann, Betty Menzel and Corinne Jacquot-Glüh, who contributed more pictures.

Anna, I will always remember your commitment as a photographer. Thank you.

Lea Maryanow, my appreciation for translating the original German book into English, Helen Bauer for her countless hours of proofreading the translation, and Alfred de Witte for his help with comparing technical terminology in the area of dog tracking.

The care of my dogs by veterinary practitioner Heidi Pohl, Markt Einersheim, has been invaluable. Thank you!

GLOSSARY

Article: This is an item that is placed on the track. The dog must find this article. The allowable shape, color and dimensions of the article are specified in the trial regulations.

Avoidance behavior: This is a reaction of the dog to a situation which he finds stressful. During a stressful trial, for example, the dog suddenly might stop and begin to eat grass.

Break in track: This is an interruption in the sequence of steps of a training track that does not allow the dog to follow the track without hesitation.

Circling: The dog leaves the exact course of the track during the track work and moves in circles in the area of the track.

Conditioning: Knowledge of what conditioning is can help the handler influence the dog's behavior. There are two types of conditioning, classical and operant. In each case, the dog's behavior can become linked to a stimulus or an action within a very short time. This link must be made repeatedly and consistently.

Confirm: This happens when the dog shows a desired behavior, and the dog handler wants to communicate that to the dog. To be most effective it should happen within two seconds through the use of treats, praise, play. etc.

Corner: This is the connecting point of two legs (straight lines) of a track, it can be right cornered or acute (between two straight lines).

Cross track: This is a second track that crosses the track to be followed. In the context of the trial regulations, a cross track is always laid later than the original track. According to the IGP, it may not intersect the track to be found at a corner of less than 60°. The cross track layer lays the cross track.

Direction of paces: This is the direction of a step in relation to the direction of the track, usually the direction of the steps points slightly sideways outwards, away from the track, with the right step sideways to the front right and with the left step sideways to the front left.

FCI Fédération Cynologique Internationale: The largest worldwide canine organization for purebred dogs and competitions.

Handler: The person leads the dog in the tracking work.

IGP Test Regulations: These are the FCI International Test Regulations for Utility Dogs from 2019.

Indicating: Desired reaction of the tracking dog when reaching an article. He can either lie down in front of the article, stand still or sit down. Another way of indicating an article is to pick it up.

Judge: The people who evaluate the performance of the dog and the handler during trials.

Leg (straight line): This is a part of a track that runs straight.

Motivation: This is the willingness of a dog to show a certain behavior.

Own track: This is a track laid by the handler himself.

Pace length: This is the distance between the steps in the direction of the track, e.g., distance between the heel of the right shoe and the toe of the left shoe.

Pace width: This is the lateral offset between the right and left step.

Punishment: This is an unpleasant consequence of an action or non-action for the dog, e.g., removal of attention, no praise or treats, blocking the lead, verbal reprimand, etc. A punishment must never lead to damage to the dog's good relationship with his handler; the requirements of the Animal Welfare Act must be strictly adhered to.

Reporting in: At a trial, the dog handler tells his name, his dog's name and the trial level to the judge. He announces his dog's behavior at articles (picking up or indicating).

Reporting out: At a trial, the dog handler declares the tracking work to be completed to the judge while the dog is in basic position. He shows the articles found.

Reward: Rewarding the dog can be done in many ways. Playing, feeding, and talking in a friendly manner are common examples. It must be positive for the dog from the dog's point of view.

Scent Pad: This is the same as the starting point, the start of the track.

Semicircle: This is a track with a semicircle design.

Scent on the track: It consists of the scent of the decomposition materials found on the grounds of the track as well as the accompanying individual scent of the tracklayer.

Starting Point: This is the beginning of the track. It is usually indicated with a rod.

Stranger's article: This is an article that has been touched and used by someone other than the handler, usually placed on a strange track (see next).

Strange Track: It is laid by a person other than the dog handler.

Track layer: The person who lays the track.

Trial: This is an event in which the performance of a dog and/or handler is assessed according to a set trial regulation.

VDH: This is the German Kennel Club, umbrella organization of breed associations and dog sport associations, member of the FCI.

Index

Connect with us

instagram

facebook

twitter

FOLLOW, LIKE, AND TAG US FOR A
CHANCE TO WIN A FREE BOOK!